The First Gozitans
(...and Ġgantija)

Revel Barker

P

Palatino Publishing

First published 2018 by Palatino Publishing
Copyright © 2018 Revel Barker

ISBN: 978-1-907841-17-0

By the same author
    Non-fiction:
*Round Up The Usual Suspects (*Editor*)*
Field of Vision
*Crying All The Way to the Bank (*Famous Trials*)*
*Publish and be Damned! (*Foreword*)*
The Last Pub In Fleet Street – A Reporter's Notebook
Għajnsielem – First and Last

    Alternative history:
The Hitler Scoop

    Fiction:
The Mayor of Montebello
The Magistrate of Montebello
The Blood Secret

The moral right to this book has been asserted. No part of this book may be reproduced, stored or transmitted in any form or by any means without the prior permission of the publishers, Palatinobooks@gmail.com

For E.A.B.
(First and last)

Revel Barker is a former Fleet Street reporter and editor, and a long-time resident on Gozo.

He was managing editor of a group of UK national newspapers and editorial adviser to international newspaper groups from Montreal to Moscow. He has been consultant to two UK universities and is now an author and a publisher (mostly of books about journalists and journalism).

He is registered in the Maltese islands as a part-time fisherman.

'The years between 5500 and 3500BC are the Mediterranean's forgotten age.'

The Making of the Middle Sea
Cyprian Broodbank

Author's note

This book is an edited, revised and greatly extended version of an earlier slim volume, *Għajnsielem, First and Last*, by the same author, which concentrated only on the history of Gozo's oldest village and newest parish.

As in the earlier work, ancient and modern documents had to be pored over, professional and amateur archaeologists were consulted, many hopefully educated assumptions were made and hopefully logical conclusions drawn.

The quote on the previous page is taken from an award-winning history (of 672-pages) by the esteemed professor of Mediterranean Archaeology at University College London.

That was the challenge for this writer, who has three or four (maybe more) 'forgotten' remnants of those very years virtually on his doorstep.

The history is there.

The evidence is there.

Forgotten, by some, perhaps. But that epoch was in fact the Age of Enlightenment that saw the start of human settlement and village life, of civilisation in Europe and, coincidentally, experienced the first known steps of Man on the Maltese archipelago – which culminated in the building of one of the archaeological wonders of the world on Gozo: the site we call *Ġgantija*.

Forgotten, but not gone – it should be understood, appreciated, marvelled at, taught in homes and in schools… and remembered. It is the Gozitan, the Maltese – and the European – birthright.

Readers requiring more detailed information about the era by professional experts in the field who are not necessarily of the same opinion(s) as this writer, are directed to the Further Reading section at the back of this book.

I am grateful to Anthony Bonanno, professor of Archaeology at the University of Malta for his help and advice and to Dr Timmy Gambin, senior lecturer in Classics & Archaeology at the same university, for his expertise in maritime and social history and for his good-humoured encouragement.

Jeremy DeBono at the National Library of Malta was, as always, a terrific help and guide.

Then I must record my thanks to a few friends, notably geologist Peter Morris and my fellow yachtsman David Youngman for their ideas and inspirational comments and arguments during the writing.

But any errors of fact (or of conjecture, or of pure fiction) herein remain this author's sole responsibility

*

Contents

Foreword: *On the origins of the species and the importance of Gozitan and Maltese prehistory.* **Page 12**

Introduction: *Considering the Who, What, Where, When, How and Why of 'the Mediterranean's forgotten age' in Neolithic Gozo and Malta* **16**

The Back-Story: *The creation of the Mediterranean Sea and the Maltese islands and the origin of the people; the Atlantis theory* **18**

Sansuna: *Folk-history and the tribe of giant women* **21**

Great Women: *The 'Fat Lady' statues that possibly inspired the folk tales; the contemporary evidence.* **25**

The Stone Age: *The history of Man's basic reliance on stone, for tools and the start of the 'new' Stone Age in civilisation.* **30**

Potted History: *The importance of ceramics in history and what it tells us. (And what we have not learnt from it.)* **32**

Stentinello: *The Sicilian connection. The demise of the 'hunter-gatherer' and the advent of farming and 'village life'. A new culture...* **36**

The End of the World: *Who the first settlers were ... What they could see... why they made the journey. The lack of evidence of fishing as an industry.* **38**

Voyage of Discovery: *What they needed to learn... Boat design, dug-out canoes and other marine craft. How they got there ...* **41**

Gozo: *The first sighting of 'three hills'.* **44**

Landfall: *What the explorers found on arrival: circumnavigating Gozo and Malta; the end of their known world. Choosing the safest inlets with the more fertile land. Changing the natural landscape.* **45**

Back to Sicily: *The necessary return trip to acquire stocks, seeds and animals, then the need to build a bigger ship in which to return.* **48**

Safe Havens: *The choice of harbours and inlets around Gozo.* **50**

Settlement: *Finding and claiming the areas of farmland that were often marked by natural boundaries.* **54**

Building with Clay: *Utilising the Sicilian tradition of 'wattle-and-daub' construction with twig walls in-filled with the island's abundant supply of clay.* **57**

Building with Bricks: *Inventing the clay 'brick' – and building with it. The 1984 discovery of a brick-built home on the Ghajnsielem road.* **60**

Geology: *Two types of ground rock – soft and hard – both suitable for building. The riddle of the 'Spork'.* **65**

Building in Stone: *The shift from clay to stone; the first use of stone for building. Erecting houses, not 'temples'. The apparent evidence of 'village life'.* **68**

The First Village: *Its discovery – walled groups of stone-built 'cottages' and tomb-caves. The serious lack of investigation and the likelihood of more of the same. The over-building of the historic sites.* **71**

The People: *The building period and comparative timeline. The industry, intelligence and innovative talents of the population. The nuclear family. Outdoor living.* **83**

The Festa: *The timing of cattle-slaughter for communal eating. The accidental creation of village 'rituals'. A casual hierarchy that might have been distinguished by occasional examples of burial with jewellery.* **88**

The 'Temple' Builders: *The attested 'care and attention' taken in domestic construction. The similarities between the building of houses and the style of the 'temples'.* **91**

Trading: *The regularity of return trips to Sicily to replenish stocks. Forms of barter, trading and employment.* **95**

Creating the Community: *Developing cooperation and collaboration among the several distinct village communities to combat times of hardship; inter-village relationships.* **98**

Council Meeting: *How decisions must necessarily have been taken. The need for a communal burial site and the reverence of the dead. The burial procedure. The emergence of a great visionary architect to build Ggantija.* **102**

What God?: *At what point in time did the settlers 'find god' – and what god was it? Different types of gods were available to them.* **113**

A Temple...?: *A place of worship. Who told them they needed to build a 'church' and attend it to communicate with their 'god'?* **119**

Priests and Oracles: *What need was there for a priest?* **124**

Animal Sacrifice: *Does the presence of an animal's skeleton found near a knife and some cinders prove that animals were sacrificed?* **128**

...Or a Mausoleum?: *Was Ġgantija the final resting-place of the dead or dying?* **132**

The Clover-leaf: *The three-leafed design as what would be the start of a building series that would later mystify the world.* **135**

Construction: *Cutting the ground plan and laying foundations... the choice of stone, finding and excavating it, and moving it.* **139**

Invention: *How they shifted the giant rocks; the invention of the 'ball-bearing' and 'the wheel'.* **143**

Ġgantija!: *The erection of a 'giant' edifice – giant rock laid upon giant rock. How this might have been achieved.* **146**

Melita: *What was happening on Malta, Gozo's sister island, meanwhile.* **160**

Archaeology: *The accidental but well-intentioned despoliation of the sites by early amateurs. The difficulties of dating. The slow response of investigation.* **166**

The End of History: *What happened next, when Gozo's pre-history stopped.* **170**

Further reading: *books and papers.* **175**

Foreword

'In the beginning'... Those *Old Testament* editors knew what they were doing by opening like that. Mankind has always been fascinated by what we nowadays refer to as 'the origin of the species': Where did we come from (and, by the way, where do we go)?

And when hard facts were unavailable, myths and theories filled in.

Thus, some are convinced that humans evolved from apes or from newts (but if that's how apes and newts evolved, why are there still apes and newts?)

Fundamentalist Judaeo-Christians believe that Man was descended from the necessarily incestuous family of Adam and Eve. And then that, on account of the Great Flood destroying all life on earth that didn't make it to the Ark, our ancestors have to be Noah's similarly inbreeding family.

In northern Europe the Celts thought their father, *Dis Pater*, was the god of the dead, rather than of birth. The Irish called him *Donn* ('the dark one') who lived on an island off the south-west coast where all his descendants were welcomed as they died.

On Gozo many believed – indeed, many were taught – that their ancestors were a race of giant women, who built temples to their (presumed but unidentified) god.

As knowledge and education intervened with the old mythology, more fables were created to subsume the new evidence which, in turn, was amended as new information became available… until the advent of compelling science proved, modified or disputed what we had been taught to believe.

This new technology is not likely to stop. What we know (and what, based on the available evidence, we think we can reasonably assume), will continue to change.

But current 'scientific' estimates of the date of a stone axe found in northern Europe vary by 220,000 years: that very imprecision indicates that archaeologists still have some way to go.

'The past', as somebody commented, 'is another country'. We don't know what we don't know about it. And what we think we know today may well be corrected tomorrow, or the next day.

This book is therefore not an archaeological treatise on Gozo and Malta. There is no shortage of worthy academic volumes on that subject.

Rather, the aim is to leave the 'temples' in the background while focussing on the agricultural community that built them: how it continued to live and how it worked.

In the beginning Man needed to learn how to survive. He needed food – and had to discover which fruits and berries were edible, and to hunt and kill specific animals for meat.

Then there was shelter – perhaps at first using tree branches and leaves, then possibly animal hides for cover and maybe a portable form of tenting, and using caves where they could be found. The life of a hunter-gatherer would be necessarily nomadic.

With the invention of organised farming – planting crops instead of searching for food, and rearing and herding animals for meat, rather than hunting for them – came the earliest signs of settlement that we can recognise to this day as 'community life'.

This was the stage of human development at which Man would first land on Gozo and Malta. They would bring with them the idea and understanding of living together (even though in the first stage it may have involved only one or two families).

And following settlement came creativity – in pottery, and, significantly, in architecture, a previously unheard of concept.

There is no evidence that the settlers could write and we do not know what language they had, but they could clearly communicate. They developed their own art, in geometrical patterns of, and on, their own cooking pots and drinking vessels… and in building design.

And the next necessity of Mankind was probably the start of some form of civilised behaviour.

These people were intelligent, inquisitive, acquisitive, artistic, and astonishingly inventive. Conditioned by the isolated but socially stable environment into which they had placed themselves, they discovered a creative genius that has amazed, and puzzled, the world.

Indeed, it has been said that the Maltese islands not only have a prehistory that is worth bothering about, but that all the prehistory worth bothering about happened on the Maltese islands.

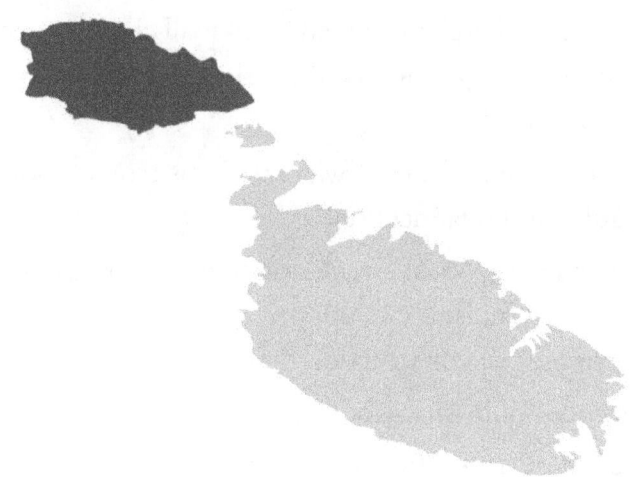

Introduction

There are more than two dozen, and maybe three dozen, Neolithic ['New Stone Age'] sites on Malta and Gozo. Nobody knows the actual figure – many of them haven't been found yet.

Not all of those that have been discovered have been excavated or examined, so there may well be surprises in store and, perhaps, some more questions. Maybe also some answers.

Meanwhile we can consider what has been found and (possibly) thoroughly examined. And it all climaxes with the construction of Ġgantija, as 'the oldest free-standing stone building on earth'.

That claim, accepted world-wide, perhaps requires some clarification and qualification.

It is free-standing – not a cave nor an extension of one, nor is it built into a hillside or supported in any way other than by its own unique construction design…

It is without doubt stone-built…

It is the oldest of a series of similar structures that would follow it.

There may yet be other buildings so far uncovered that pre-date it, but unless or until that happens it is a claim that will endure for the future histories of Mankind.

What we are not 100 per cent sure about is *why* it was built.

What we do know (or think we know) is *who* the strange and dedicated people that history describes as 'the temple builders' were.

We know, with a fair degree of certainty, *where* they came from and, give or take a century or so, *when* they arrived.

We can theorise, with applied logic, about *how* they arrived (first on Gozo and then on Malta).

We can speculate about *why* they came.

We know *where* on the islands they settled, because they left evidence of it – some of it in shards of pottery and, later, much of it in stone.

We can see for ourselves some examples of *what* they built, first in mud, then in clay brick, and finally in stone.

We can undoubtedly identify some of the sites *where* they built monuments.

And we can deduce *how* they built them.

Most archaeology has concentrated on the so-called religious sites – the majestic 'ritual' buildings and the cemeteries – while tending to neglect the secular, the actual settlements of the people who did the building and excavating.

In general, the only domestic sites that have been thoroughly explored are those 'temples' that had previously been used for housing, or that had been occupied as accommodation after the 'temples' were for some reason abandoned.

That seems unfortunate. It is surely at least as important to know *how* those isolated prehistoric people lived and worked, as to stand back and marvel at *what* they built.

But we should be grateful that they did it.

*

The Back-Story

Through researching the history of the Maltese islands as a whole (or at least simply as a pair of small but significant islands) one learns of the geological fact that, at one time, the entire Mediterranean area was land-locked, at Gibraltar, with lakes within and possibly paths and even (perhaps) 'cart tracks' crossing through Gozo and Malta from Sicily to Libya.

Archaeological evidence also suggests that there were undomesticated animals inhabiting the 'mountains' (which would be all that was left visible, after the Atlantic Ocean burst in and flooded the plains).

These apparently included red deer, bear, fox and wolf.

Much earlier than that, there is also archaeological evidence of *Pleistocene* species [maybe 250,000 years earlier] such as dwarf elephants and miniature hippopotamuses that had presumably adapted to their diet and to the environment.

The Atlantic breakthrough is widely understood to have been the 'flood' in the story of Noah's Ark as related in the Bible's *Genesis* and, in variations, in the *Quran*.

Before that, the basin we nowadays know as the Mediterranean Sea was a mostly arid area with a series of mainly volcanic mountains whose summits would become islands and hills as the deluge roared in.

Perhaps the miniature species of giant animals were among those that missed the boat.

Many Maltese (and some outsiders) believe that their archipelago, being former hilltops centrally and therefore importantly situated between Europe and Africa, is (or was) the 'lost city of Atlantis' whose inhabitants would besiege ancient Athens in a totally fictional story by Plato (who claimed it to be a factual account).

Then the Greek poet Eumalos of Cyrene wrote in the 8th Century BC that…

> 'the summit of Mount Atlas, which was situated in the middle of the island Atlantika was not submerged. This summit of Mount Atlas has preserved the name of Ogyge from that of its last king, and it is in fact this circumstance why we still know as Ogygia that island which still exists between Libia and Sicily; it is nothing more than the summit of Mount of Atlantika.'

Several other ancient authors, including Callimachus, Herodotus, Hesiod and Diodorus Siculus have identified 'Ogygia' as Gozo, the island of Calypso and Ulysses.

Surely Plato and so many forgotten writers can't all be wrong?

But the clear evidence is that the islands are entirely made of rocks consisting solely of compacted corals that were forced upwards, out of the bottom of the sea, about 20 million years ago. This was caused by the movement of the giant earth plates of Europe and Africa – and later additionally aided by the great flood that created the Mediterranean Sea some 12,000 years ago.

There are more recent suggestions that Malta was first inhabited by giant temple-building people from 'outer space'… not, as one might perhaps expect, from Mars, but apparently originating from Sirius, the brightest star in the night sky.

They chose Malta, from all the alternative options on earth, because of its abundance of limestone, which 'has the capacity to absorb, store, and transfer energy.'

Even that proposition seems to make sense, to some people.

But all this is a digression from the true (or at least credible) story of 'the temple builders', and – maybe with the exception of the space-invader theory – perhaps worthy of a totally different investigation.

Sansuna

One popular version of a Gozitan folk tale says that all the enormous stones of the megalithic remains at Ġgantija [mega = great; lithos = stone, in Greek] were brought to their present sites by a single giant woman named *Sansuna*. According to the story this incredibly strong woman carried massive blocks of rock on her head from ta' Ċenċ to Għajnsielem, thence to Qala and on to Xagħra.

Sansuna – her name (surely no more than a happy coincidence) is a Maltese female translation of the name *Samson* – lived on a diet of honey and of broad beans that she kept in her pocket.

She carried a baby in a sling over her shoulder and used to spin flax as she walked, bearing her heavy load.

At times she would balance the rock with her hand so as not to let it fall – a seemingly insignificant detail that was probably added to make the unlikely story seem more realistic: easier to picture in the imagination of an audience.

Some time before embarking on the building project at Ġgantija (which would take her one whole day, from sunrise to sunset) she had brought a huge rock to Qala to use as a stool on which she would sit and spin while guarding her field of broad beans. Known as the Qala *menhir* [standing stone], Sansuna's seat is about three metres tall.

Some variants of the tale mention that she was one-and-a-half times taller than the stone. It is said that she also built *Id-Dura tal-Mara* ['the Woman's Hut'] at ta' Ċenċ, where she, and her stones, came from.

Another version of the story, doubtless intended to be more credible, is that the building was not the work of one solo multi-tasking giant woman, but of a whole race of them who were the first inhabitants of the island. Not far from St Francis' church in Victoria is a place called *Il-Ġemgħa tal-Ġganti* [the Giants' Council] where all the women used to meet.

And then, just as suddenly as they had appeared, the tribe of amazons vanished, or died out.

*

Those, at least, are the Ġgantija legends. Gozo abounds in similar fantastic stories: from the giant woman or women (circa 5000BC) to the nymph Calypso entertaining Ulysses for seven years at Ramla Bay in Homer's *Odyssey* (around 1200BC)... even to a Biblical 'Golden Calf' brought over by Hebrews after their eviction from Jerusalem that was buried for safety and abandoned on their deportation from Gozo (AD1494), then discovered and reburied by a local farmer who died under torture while refusing to reveal its whereabouts.

Stories like this were collected and written for the first time by a Jesuit priest, Fr Emmanuel Magri, between 1902 and 1906 while he was rector of the Gozo Seminary. He called them *l-għerf bla miktub*, meaning 'the unwritten learning'. Perhaps, because they were being related and published by a priest, they were taken by some unsophisticated people as being gospel.

Whatever, they were the tales that grandmothers used to (and perhaps still do) love to tell.

While some of the legends have at least vague historical dating, the origins of all of them are lost in time. We know, for example, when there was an émigré Jewish community on Gozo.

We know that the Gozitan connection with Calypso – a mythical character in a poem – is, at best, fanciful.

As for the giant women …

*

*Female figurine in clay discovered at Tarxien.
(About 6cm tall)*

*

Great Women

Where the history doesn't exist, it sometimes needs to be invented, or at least to be assumed (hopefully both logically and most likely). It is what professional archaeologists do to this day; story-tellers, the popular creators of what would become folk-tales in later years, would have done the same. And ancient Gozitans, when first exploring the magnificent structure that would become known as Ġgantija, must have been impressed by the recurring number of surviving statues of big (that is, fat) women inside the building or elsewhere close by, and of a contemporary era.

The statues were mostly small – many are described as 'figurines' – but the figures depicted are generally obese.

Interestingly (and perhaps importantly), none of the human statues exhibits identifiably male characteristics, while others are quite obviously female, often with rounded breasts and buttocks and occasionally clearly identifiable genital areas. Some of the statues are impossible to categorise by gender: they may have depicted men, but when dressed they wore pleated skirts, not trousers.

Easier, in that case, for later generations to assume that they were a tribe of women. Perhaps, then, these were carved in recognition of the people (or person) who moved the stones and built the 'temples'…

The stones were massive – modern experts reckon that it would take at least 50 'normal' people to move any of the biggest rocks, then to place one stone on top of another…

So, the builders must have been giants.

The hard grey coralline limestone was certainly similar to stones seen in abundance at ta' Ċenċ, so perhaps they were carried from there…

The staple diet of the prehistoric population of Gozo could very likely have been broad beans and honey…

There is also some actual archaeological evidence of early inhabitants spinning flax to make linen…

A few plausible facts are introduced to give the narrative credibility.

They all seem to fit.

There is nobody around who can dispute any of it. That is the way legends are born.

Sadly, there is not a whiff of evidence to support any of the Sansuna tradition.

It is true that even today we hear unwitnessed stories of farmers who unearth skeletal bones of 'giants', sometimes reportedly as great as three metres (ten feet) in height, that they quickly disperse before anyone else sees them because, at the very least, if their field became 'a site of archaeological interest' it would almost certainly put a stop to ploughing.

There is of course a readily available explanation for this: rather than dying out, the giant woman and her fellow amazons interbred with the local population (a tribe of only women would not have survived beyond a single generation… and Sansuna's babe-in-arms must have come from somewhere) and that the 'giant gene' gradually diminished.

But how much height and strength would a solitary woman, even a tribe of women, need to have possessed at the start, in order to have been up to the task of moving and positioning the massive megaliths of Ġgantija?

Worse, for the *folkloristi*, dating of various statues sculpted before the temples were built – and they were all clearly of women – shows there were no signs of gigantism as (presumably) the sign of an attractive or at least important female figure.

The apparent fixation with female obesity came after or during the 'temple building' era, not before.

Worse still, archaeologists have found skeletons – hundreds of them – that are contemporary with the building of Ġgantija.

Both sexes are all of 'normal' height, and of Sicilian ancestry.

*

Part of a 'giant' statue from Tarxien. The complete figure would have stood about 2m tall. But does it depict a male or female subject?

The 'Sleeping Lady' found at Hal Saflieni. Although only 7cm long, the detail is delicate. Long hair, with a headband, naked to the waist, ample breasts, a slim waist, and large thighs in a pleated skirt.

There is reasonable cause to believe that the builders were regular prehistoric people, at least some of whom lived in the area of Gozo that is today on the edges of Għajnsielem, where early settlers had started construction in bricks of clay, before (or even while) progressing to working with stone.

And rather than its being built by Sansuna in a single day, archaeologists say that construction of Ġgantija took at least 600, and maybe more than 1,000 years. So, if not giant women, who were these builders?

*

The Stone Age

The latter years of Prehistory are usually divided into the Stone Age, Bronze Age and Iron Age (there are other subdivisions going back millions of years that do not concern us here).

The Stone Age is divided into three epochs: Eo-lithic [*dawn-*] and Palaeo-lithic [*ancient-*], when the crudest forms of stone implements were used — then Neo-lithic [*new-*], which marks the beginning of recognisable 'village' life: farming, the making of pottery, using flint to replace hard stone tools and of obsidian glass as a scraping instrument.

Although these changes may have occurred singly, elsewhere, it was in Sicily, in Stentinello near Syracuse, that they all came together as a completely new culture.

This was not an evolution of the Palaeolithic age: it was a sudden stop and a re-start. It was the New [Neo] Stone Age. Hence its name. (Archaeologists have sub-divided it again, to cover the different ages of 'temple-building'; it makes it easier for them, but more difficult for the layman, to follow.)

The New Stone Age ran until the Bronze Age (which was a late starter as an historic epoch on Gozo, where there was no metal of any kind). But since the people were still Neolithic and most decidedly prehistoric, that is, 'before history', what do we know about them?

Monoliths used in the building into a hillside of a 'temple' at Göbekli Tepe in south-east Turkey, 11,000 years ago.

Cave-dwelling – Italy

Potted History

Gozitan history starts with the presumption that, at the beginning of the story, the island (and also the island of Malta) was uninhabited.

The archipelago's nearest neighbours were northern Africa – Libya to the south and Tunisia to the west, both about 180 miles, or 290km, away – and Sicily, 58 miles (93km) to the north.

Any of them could have 'discovered' Gozo and Malta, and it is perfectly possible that they did (although there is no indication of African visitation). So, based solely on the evidence of ancient pieces of pottery found there, archaeologists have deduced that, without any doubt, the first actual 'settlers' were Sicilian. Furthermore – also based on the evolution of pottery styles – they have deduced that Gozo was settled first, shortly before Malta.

They have dated the arrival at some time around 5000BC. This is an arbitrary 'nearest-round-figure' date, presumably because although the date of manufacture of a piece of pottery can be fixed fairly precisely, it doesn't mean that it was discarded or abandoned in the same year – or even in the same century. Or (sometimes importantly) even in the place where it was made.

It is therefore readily accepted that the first habitation could have been established 100, or maybe 500, or even 1,000 years earlier.

Pottery fascinates archaeologists, first, because it seems to last for ever; and second, because no two potters' work is ever identical. Different tribes or communities tended to develop their own individual styles, and also their patterns, often geometrical, which were etched into the clay using sticks, shells, fingernails or animal bones. Sometimes they crimped the tops or lips of vessels with their fingertips or with sea shells.

Pottery types varied with innovation and with 'fashion', in that individual generations of families would stick to a certain traditional style that successive generations amended or improved. For example, at some stage it became clear that a 'vase' type of vessel with a pinched neck would be more practical for carrying liquids than a bowl would. And handles were also often redesigned for convenience.

If one looks at the range of design available in any modern pottery shop, there are probably few shapes that had not been made at some time on prehistoric Gozo or Malta. Only the thickness and final glazing would be significantly different, because ancient potters had to mix their rough clay and design their own (open fire) kilns.

Histories of pottery often seem to overwhelm the study of the histories of how civilisation itself evolved and the housing in which it lived. It is rarely the only remaining evidence. Pottery may unlock some of the secrets of prehistoric life, but its relics are usually found among domesticity. The way that the potters lived, rather than the items that they crafted, is what we would like to know about.

After all, the potters (like every other member of any community) needed shelter, somewhere to live. Following the choice of a place to settle, this meant a hut, a house or a cottage. It had to be built, which involved the identification and collection of materials, the clearing and marking out of a site, the foundations and flooring, the framing, plaiting, filling, weatherproofing, and roofing…

Potters needed to be fed, which necessitated farming – choosing a field, clearing it of stones, sowing seeds, weeding, and harvesting, then grinding crops… There was also the procuring, breeding, tending and herding of animals, including cows (and bulls), sheep, goats and pigs. And then the slaughtering of them in order to supplement a basic cereal diet.

Somebody had to find, plant, grow and collect and cook vegetables…

They would need clothing, so the hides and the sheepskin would have to be scraped, cured and cut to shape… and perhaps the wool would be woven. Somebody would invent button-type fastenings.

Obviously they required water, not only for pottery but also for life. There had to be water-carrying people (and something in which they could carry it), then water conservation for the dry summer months – so, dams and cisterns, which had to be dug out of the permeable rock and lined with clay.

And they needed boats, with crews and navigators for trading that required international contact.

The histories of pottery certainly provide clues, but they don't tell anything like the whole story.

*

Stentinello

From these histories we learn that a piece of pottery found in Gozo indicates that the earliest settlers came from (or came ashore with pottery that had been made in) the village of Stentinello, just north of Syracuse in south-eastern Sicily, and home of the first signs anywhere on earth of a Neolithic culture.

In the era of early decorated pottery it stood out as what would become known as 'impressed ware' – geometrical patterns, possibly copied from the natural pattern on sea shells, etched into the moist clay, usually round the widest part, before firing – and also recognised by unique designs, from hemispherical bowls, some like soup dishes, to others like mixing bowls, and flasks with a short, shaped, neck.

One small complication is that similar pieces have been found elsewhere on Sicily, and even in Calabria, suggesting that it was widely traded.

Nevertheless, the pottery on Gozo has been identified as having originated in Stentinello and can be dated to around the fifth millennium BC, so it is a fair guess that the people did, too… or from somewhere not far away. In which case the incoming settlers were a relatively, and remarkably, advanced community of Sicilians.

Rather than depending for sustenance on hunting wild

animals and collecting uncultivated fruit (the 'hunter-gatherers'), they had learnt to plant and grow their own food and to breed and rear animals – first, sheep and goats and, later, cattle and pigs. Instead of living in caves they built huts and created small 'village' communities that they sometimes bordered with stone walls or ditches.

Moving on from relying on hard rock or flakes of flint for their major tools, they had discovered the use of much sharper obsidian glass from volcanic lava. They also made axes by polishing basalt and greenstone rocks.

It appears that the Stentinello inhabitants had travelled a bit before settling in Sicily, and – being both inquisitive and intelligent – had learnt snippets of knowledge from other communities that they combined to create their unique and rounded 'culture' which was actually the starting point of 'civilisation' in Europe, as we know it.

This culture would eventually spread – distinguished primarily by copies of its pottery – around the shores of the Mediterranean, obviously signifying trading and friendship or unity (or at least a lack of aggression) between the different habitations. And this was the culture that they were going to bring to 'Gozo'.

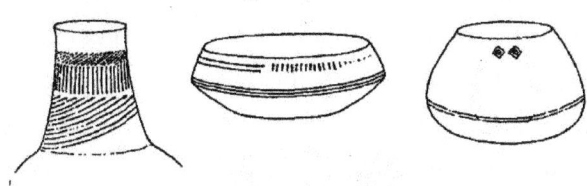

The End of the World

Inland farmers working on hillsides in the south of Sicily would have been able to see that there was land across the sea; on a clear day it was just about visible, maybe even from as far north as Etna – but certainly from the area around Stentinello. Therefore the south coast of their island was not, as some might have believed, the end of the world – there was land beyond it (maybe the actual end).

All the inhabitants of the island at that time were known as Sicani – in that they were the first Sicilian people to have an identifiable tribal name. There are no signs of any warfare among the people nor, at that time on the largest island in the Mediterranean, should there have been any shortage of land.

The frequent but unpredictable, and therefore dangerous, eruptions of Mount Etna, with red hot lava pouring randomly down its slopes and burning and burying people's homes and fields, may have been truly frightening… but then, those in the vicinity could simply have moved away.

Religious persecution, which in later history would become an understandable reason for emigration, is unlikely if only because there is no knowledge of any extant religion during this period of history – even though modern man has made the fantastic and entirely unsupported presumption that they were 'sun worshippers'.

Or that they worshipped 'Mother Earth'… or both.

Mankind's seemingly insatiable desire for exploration might appear to be the most likely motivation.

They went 'because it was there'…

*

Maritime navigation was very much in its infancy, and the crossing of large expanses of sea would be difficult, and perhaps considered impossible. So any communication and exploration would be restricted to linking shores that were visible, each from the other, or simply confined to coastal voyages.

Although Stentinello is on the coast and its people's great difference in knowledge and culture from the rest of Sicily suggests that its earliest inhabitants may have been newcomers who arrived by sea, and although it is perfectly feasible that some farmers were also part-time fishermen (as is the case with a few Gozitans even today), it is perhaps astonishing to note that professional archaeologists finely sieving the ancient sites have found no evidence of fish being eaten by pre-historic settlers on the Maltese islands – nor even anywhere in pre-historic Sicily.

They have found relics of spinning and weaving, of small hand-tools and even of decorative beads and pendants and coat buttons.

Sea shells were occasionally used for adornment and for

shaping the rims of some styles of pottery (so it may well have been likely that the flesh would have been eaten, at least experimentally).

Surprisingly, if they speared, netted, or caught fish on a hook and line, there is no trace of any even rudimentary fishing tackle.

However, as archaeologists are given to saying, absence of evidence is not the same as evidence of absence. They may yet turn up some proof of fishing as an industry or a pastime or as food – it just hasn't been found yet.

(And modern isotope and trace element analysis of skeletons of the first settlers show that they mostly ate meat or vegetables. Trace elements that would be left by eating copious amounts of fish or seafood are noticeably absent.)

But any full-time fishermen, if there were indeed such craftsmen or even hobbyists working the coastal waters of southern Sicily, would have been unaware of the landfall to the south because the range of visibility from sea-level is generally estimated to be only about three miles.

The first problem, then, for the would-be adventurers on their hill-slopes would be how to get to it, and from whom they could seek advice and knowledge.

It could not have been a hasty decision for the farming families to have taken.

*

Voyage of Discovery

Nothing at all is known about the type of craft used by local boatmen of the period, but the Egyptians had already made vessels out of reeds in a stem-to-stern shape that would be recognised today. And the (earlier) populating of previously uninhabited islands such as Crete – and even the distribution of identifiably Sicilian pottery and flint – proves that there was some sort of maritime movement – so there is no reason to assume that Sicilian sailors – who had access to the same sort of reeds as the Egyptians – could not have developed their own style of seaworthy ship from locally available materials.

Before 5450BC (wood can be carbon-dated fairly precisely) mainland Italians had invented a dugout canoe – as was discovered near Rome in 1994(AD). Ten metres (33ft) long with a beam of about one metre, it had been carved from a single oak. It was seaworthy, but would have needed a crew of ten people with short paddles to propel it. Even then, an oar-driven voyage from southern Sicily to Gozo would have taken three days and nights. But nobody knows what the Sicilians were using.

They had pottery at hand and could easily have realised that a cup or bowl would float. Perhaps they made something in the fashion that we nowadays would recognise as a 'coracle' – a round and hemispherical vessel made by woven branches and possibly lined with animal skin to make it watertight. Maybe they made dug-out canoes from the tall local oak or pine trees, and later used strips or planks of wood to make far larger craft based on a similar design. Without the knowledge or ability to bend stronger timber the shape would need to become oval: more ship-shape.

By applying basic common sense they would very soon have realised the advantage of adding at least one sail (if they had something more stable than a canoe) to assist or relieve their oars or paddles.

The adventurous farmers first needed to build a seaworthy boat, or somehow to acquire one, and then to learn how to sail it. They would have to learn basic navigation (by the sun, the moon or the stars) because the distant island would not be visible from sea level for most of the voyage – and without some understanding of maintaining a course they could have sailed straight past the island on their horizon.

If they had had the benefit of learning from a sailor who had been out at night and who had worked out how to find his way home, they might have known that by sitting in the bow of the ship and keeping *Polaris*, the North Star, at the head of the mast they would have sailed due south and stayed on course... literally, an early lesson in 'astral navigation'. They may have been told that, in an otherwise cloudless sky, there often appears to be a cloud above a piece of land, making it easier to find.

As farmers they would have known about the dominant north-west wind and also about other winds from the north and the north-east. In the spring and autumn the *Sirocco*, blowing from the south, from the Sahara, could make their voyage arduous and uncomfortable, with visibility greatly reduced because of the amount of sand in the air.

Experienced seamen may have told them that the predominant current is very slight and to the south-east but that there can often be sudden swells, making the sea what modern sailors describe as 'lumpy'. Local mariners may have known about that.

Forewarned, the farmers somehow got themselves equipped and organised, waited for a time when the weather was calm enough for safety, but the wind was strong enough to drive them in the right direction, and sailed off… into the unknown. They could quite possibly have completed the journey in one long late spring or early autumn day – although they would not have been aware of that when they embarked on their voyage.

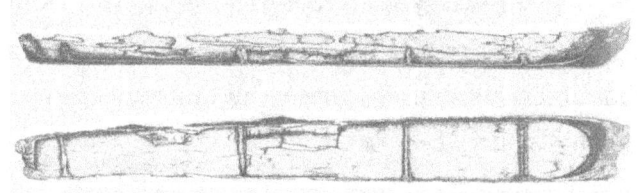

Starboard elevation and plan of a dugout canoe found in the Neolithic village of La Marmotta, on Lake Bracciano.

Gozo

Closing on the island that would one day become known as 'Gozo' (perhaps while still 20 or so miles distant) they would first have seen the three hills that would later become seemingly significant as landmarks, but which would quickly merge unidentifiably into the skyline of hilltop plateaux.

Then – sailing on and obviously discovering Malta beyond it – having circumnavigated the two islands (four, if you include Comino and Fifla), and finding nothing in sight beyond them except miles of vast, empty sea, there was no reason to venture further.

They would have noted impossibly steep or vertical uninviting limestone cliffs on the west of the islands and gentler slopes, and rocky beaches along the east and, having finally reached the limits of their known world, they would have returned to rest in the apparent safe havens of the islands that they had logged along their way.

And, apart from two massive deep natural harbours and a few narrow coves on Malta, the safest and most comfortably appealing inlets they discovered would have been on the more fertile island of Gozo.

*

Landfall

To the first arriving Sicilian (perhaps at some time between 6000-5600BC), the overall landscape of the island would not have been much different from the open countryside where it can still be found today: with the exceptions that it would obviously have been totally unoccupied and unbuilt, but also having many small copses of pine, ash and evergreen oak ('holly oak') trees.

Beyond and beside the fertile valleys was mostly open scrubland and *maquis*, bushes and low growth plants that may have included hawthorn, and carob, fig and almond trees with green shrubs, aromatic herbs, and bunchgrasses, which can be found elsewhere today, even in poor or dry soil anywhere in the Mediterranean.

After mooring safely according to the wind and then venturing inland, the intrepid explorers must have been disappointed to find that there were no indigenous 'domestic' animals (nor even wild animals that could become domesticated) and no arable crops.

Worse, although there were stones everywhere on the topsoil, and there was 'chert', which was considered to be an inferior type of flint and could be used as a very primitive form of axe, there were no 'superior' rock types.

They knew that they needed flint and obsidian that were

already being used in the Stentinello area and would be required to make the variety of stone tools that they would need for farming.

Even if they had embarked, first, on a simple voyage of discovery – an expedition to see what was there, rather than having emigrated blindly – we can assume that they would have brought plenty of the essentials of life with them. But for continuous habitation they would need more of the same – and it would have to be imported from back home, in Sicily.

The land could be made habitable. This rock-strewn and uninhabited island presented a blank canvas on which the explorers could envisage creating something new.

It had a few decent harbours, some safer than others in the persistent but inconsistent north-west wind. There was a decent depth of fertile soil on gently sloping plains (from which the surface stones would need to be removed) and there was fresh water in a few places. It could support a small number of small communities.

But they were still faced with the fact that to acquire the very basic necessities for a new life… getting hard materials for making tools, like flint (from the Monti Iblei mountain range in south-east Sicily) and the sharper obsidian glass (from Lipari, a small volcanic island off the northern coast)… acquiring a breeding stock of farm animals – cattle, sheep, pigs, goats, and perhaps a donkey or two… plus the wherewithal to plant crops… All this would require a return voyage to Sicily.

And if they were going to sail back to stock up and return to create a community, the first thing they would need to do back home would be to build a bigger and more sturdy ship.

Something convinced them that it would all be worthwhile.

Was it simply the irresistible urge to create something – effectively as their own small homeland – completely new?

Or was it also because they were overwhelmed by the singular beauty of the place… looking from the south coast, across the narrow channel into the vivid Blue Lagoon on Comino, or perhaps watching the sun set between the dramatic cliffs at Xlendi?

Southern Sicily had nothing to compare with such scenic splendour.

Whatever their motivation, the decision was made – there is archaeological evidence to support this – to sail home, build that big vessel, fill it, and sail back to create a new home: to them, a new world.

The introduction of farming and of cattle and pigs, and then the start of housing development, was going to mean making changes to the landscape of the islands that would never stop.

*

Back to Sicily

Even if – in spite of the lack of evidence – there were enterprising local fishermen, even some who had progressed to building big boats, large enough, and stable enough, say, to haul big tuna on board, they would have had nothing that could float safely with a cargo of cattle, pigs, goats and sheep. The new craft would need to be a veritable Noah's Ark… maybe a huge raft, with planks and cattle pens on its decks, tree trunks beneath to ensure stability and possibly long, grouped and bundled shafts of light hollow bamboo for better flotation. Or simply a set of dug-out canoes strapped side by side…

Two or three thousand years later they would have invented a vessel that would not look out of place in a Maltese fishing harbour today. And they were so proud of it that drawings were etched on a megalith at Tarxien in Malta. (Or perhaps it was how the ship was first sketched and designed…)

But, long before getting to this stage, the realisation of the need for an original design, the arguments over different possible options and then final agreement, building and sea trials, would have taken a considerable amount of time and doubt. Was it all worthwhile…? Yes – it obviously was.

So eventually, confident and fully laden, they set sail, back to…

They must have given the place a name.

The Phoenicians, when they took over, thought of the island as being circular and would call it *Gwl* [pronounced Goll] after the shape of their round merchant ships.

The Greeks would call it *Gaulus*, their word for the same sort of vessel.

Whatever the newcomers called it, their island would go through several name-changes during the following seven millennia, including Gaulos, Gaudes, Gaudos, Ghawdex and Gaudisium, before becoming … 'Gozo'.

*

Safe Havens

While the story, as recounted here, may be understood as relating to one group of people – perhaps only to one extended family or small group of friends – the strong likelihood is that other, possibly completely unconnected, families or syndicates were doing exactly the same thing, at roughly the same time, and quite possibly disembarking on the island in different places.

The oldest pieces of Sicilian pottery found anywhere on the Maltese islands were near a huge cave, separated into two by a natural column (and later by a man-made wall) at *il-Mixta* on the Għajn Abdul plateau (*Għajn* means spring or fountain), near what is now San Lawrenz on the north-west of the island.

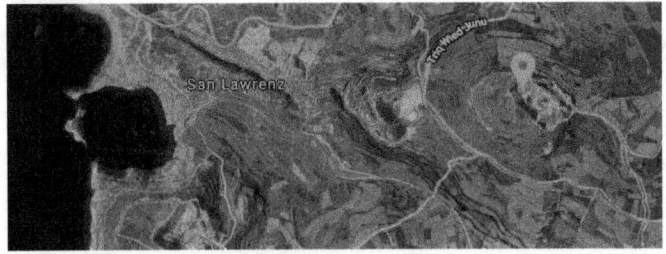

Dwejra and Il-Mixta cave (Google Satellite)

This site (now mostly destroyed by modern quarrying) is above Dwejra Bay, which must have appeared an attractive harbour for the first arriving explorers, with its overwhelming cliffs that formed almost a complete circle, and one small area where they could make land. A giant rock (later known as Fungus Rock) at the entrance would protect them from any except the west winds. And it had the *ghajn* flowing down to it as a source of fresh water.

Contemporary voyagers would have discovered Xlendi, a fjord-like bay on the south-west of the island between spectacularly sheer cliffs with several caves to serve as shelters. Originally a single extraordinarily deep inland cave, its roof had collapsed through erosion. At the point in history when the first adventurers would have been coming ashore the natural harbour extended inland to the area that today is a car park and would have provided vital defence against the prevailing north-west and westerly winds.

There was fresh water a few hundred yards uphill at what is now appropriately called Fontana. And there were more caves in the cliffs above it, near Santa Luċija and Taċ-Ċawla.

Mgarr ix-Xini

Mġarr ix-Xini, on the south coast, would possibly also have extended a short way further inland than it does today and there were caves there, too (most of them by now collapsed). This would have been the safest harbour on the island, the major problem perhaps being that it was too narrow for any but the smallest boats to manoeuvre.

Its incoming settlers might have made their homes at the top of the hill where there were natural freshwater wells at what is now Xewkija, a name derived from the Arabic word *Xewk*, meaning thistle or thorn. Or they may have settled at ta' Ċenċ (which would later feature importantly, if only in the story of Sansuna), or at Ta'Maziena on the Sannat road.

It is likely that the anvil-shaped Marsalforn bay would also have attracted sailors – for its harbour once also extended sufficiently far inland to offer protection, although its mouth was wide open to both of the often violent north-westerly *Majjistral* and north-easterly *Gregale* winds.

They could have easily beached their craft on the wide stretch of red sand at the foot of a rich and fertile valley now called Ramla il-Ħamra – 'the red sandy beach'. There were caves in the rocky cliffs above it, including the complex labyrinth that would later be assigned to 'Calypso'. There was a fresh water stream running into the bay.

This magnificent curving bay also faced due north: it was unlikely to be chosen as a permanent anchorage, despite the attractive setting that would become known as the most beautiful beach in the Maltese archipelago, although there were plenty more natural and habitable caves further inland, in Xagħra.

In fact, the pioneer settlers would be spoilt for choice in deciding at which point to make their historic landfall...However, there is no remaining visible evidence of any early built habitation in or near any of these harbours.

It is assumed that these, and other, sites would originally have been temporary cave shelters, as distinct from any permanent purpose-built domestic development using stone. The caves could be chipped out to increase both width and depth, and perhaps continued outside by a form of 'wattle and daub' – twig and clay – extension.

Evidence has been found, well inland, of pottery-making near the caves at Santa Luċija (locally made but following the style of Stentinello) and there are remains of what appears to be 'a substantial stone wall', at Taċ-Ċawla, near Victoria (Rabat) which suggests both some form of building expertise and also longer-term occupation, even if not of actual house-building.

But we know for sure that on the south coast, at some stage, the new arrivals started building houses...

*

Settlement

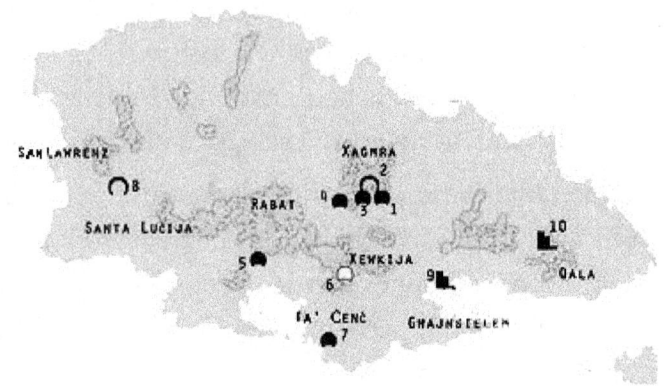

1 – Ġgantija
2 – Ta'Għejzu
3 – Xagħra Circle
4 – Santa Verna
5 – Ta' Marziena

6 – Xewkija
7 – Il-Borġ ta' l-Imramma
8 – Il-Mixta
9 – Tal Qigħan & L-Imrejżbiet
10 – Qala Menhir

Having landed at what is now Mġarr, a wide and shallow bay in which they could safely haul up and beach their boats – sheltered for most of the summer but wide open to the strong southerly *Xlokk* or *Sirocco* winds that leave a deposit of fine sand carried from the Sahara – they eventually trekked uphill, following a valley of bamboos with fresh water flowing along it, until reaching an area of fairly level high ground that would be suitable for farming... once the trees and surface stones had been cleared.

There were, and still are, also caves in the rock-face above and beyond this bay, extending as far east as *Qala* [meaning 'sheltered cove']. And the pioneers had probably made short-term use of them before making their inland ascent in search of suitable sustainable agricultural land.

The wide, gently undulating plateau that they had chosen had a natural border at Mgarr ix-Xini to the west and, to the north, the 200-foot rock escarpment that is now marked by the Nadur belvederes (from where the perennial supply of fresh water for their valley emanated) and the steep slope to the sea at the south.

On the north side of that narrow escarpment was another wide and verdant plain that was adopted for farming, probably by a separate group. It was also fed by a watercourse from the Nadur hilltop.

This one extended in the north to the limits of Xaghra, where Ġgantija would eventually be built. A few oval mud-huts would be built here and reservoirs cut out of the groundrock. It would become known, later, as *In-Nuffara*.

On the other side of the island, yet more explorers who ventured inland, perhaps moving from the Calypso grotto's temporary seaside shelter at Ramla to a gently sloping open area suitable for farming, were doing the same thing at what would become Santa Verda (on the Xaghra plateau).

It would therefore appear more than likely that most of the incoming shiploads of adventurers were finding, claiming, and occupying individual areas of farmland – most of it marked by natural borders.

There was, however, no domestic shelter on any of these plateaux. If they wanted to live and to farm there, the settlers would need to build their own homes.

*

Building with Clay

Creating some at least crude form of domesticity had to be the priority, and happily beneath the useful topsoil they found an abundance of blue clay that could be used for 'wattle-and-daub' building: panels of woven tree branches or bamboo shoots [the 'wattle'], in-filled with the clay [the 'daub'].

Because Gozo's archaeology concentrates more on the religious than on the domestic orientation of the explorers, our knowledge of their first primitive construction techniques relies heavily on the experience that they brought with them from Sicily.

It exhibits the earliest type of architecture and planning that would stand them in such admirable and impressive stead throughout the next few thousand years.

First would come the pacing out of distances and then the cutting of soil down to rock level, and then infilling with small stones as a foundation to prevent the upward creeping degradation of the walls from damp ground.

Next came the collection of tall strong timbers and perhaps sturdy bamboo as vertical support beams secured in holes chipped into the rock, then sticks, reeds and twigs that could be inter-laced as a structural skeleton for the walls.

After that, some sort of twine or grass or cordage to hold it all in shape. And, finally, would be the infilling with that plentiful resource of blue clay

Practically and logically – and if these first settlers had not brought both practicality and logic with them they would acquire both, soon enough – they would have built on escarpments that provided easiest access to the clay strata, and thereby the shortest distance to transport it (perhaps after being quarried by hand). Even a small hut would require several tons for plastering into the walls to reach a waterproof and windproof quality.

At all times there was also the need for water – in vast quantities – with which to work in the straw and twigs to strengthen and smooth the daub.

And when, or while, the walls were being finished, a roof: perhaps a form of thatched straw laid across longer timbers and, again, probably weatherproofed with clay.

All this – the marking out and cutting of earth, the gathering of branches, planting of support beams, crushing and grinding the foundations, collecting big stones for wall footings and hearths, weaving reeds and daubing the framework – probably to a minimum six-inch (15cm) thickness for insulation – must have been both time consuming and labour intensive.

Carriage, of water and of clay, would have been the biggest problem. These builders had nothing that even remotely resembled a wheel-barrow. Nor would they ever invent one.

We might imagine a pair of leather buckets on a yoke: and if the carriers had carted the clay to the site first, the buckets might have been relatively waterproofed already.

But, working together, as they would learn to do even if they hadn't already discovered the benefits of doing so, with both sexes and maybe friends and children able to assist in some way, they could in all probability erect a small habitable 'mud hut' in about two weeks… before starting on the next one. They appear to have built in separate family units: one hut per household, without realising the obvious benefits of saving at least the building of one wall by creating 'semi-detached' or even 'terraced' housing. Nevertheless, a form of annex or extension would have been built on to some of the dwellings to allow for vital storage and as all-weather workrooms, perhaps for spinning, weaving and preparing hides during the rainy season.

In all probability, any sort of building work would have been a seasonal occupation: most likely restricted to spring and summer to allow the clay to dry out and to expose the cracks that would predictably occur in it, requiring re-plastering.

Yet another factor, and this might have influenced the scheduling patterns for much later building development, was the need to avoid the seasons that farmers would require for such agricultural necessities as sowing, harvesting and lambing.

A house built in this fashion could be expected to last for 20 or 30 years before starting to disintegrate – by which time the next generation would have completed a new wave of individually designed wattle and daub 'mud huts'.

*

Building with Bricks

This they doubtless did… before realising that the quick-drying and hardening of the clay would allow them to fashion 'bricks' out of it, dry them in the searingly hot summer sunshine, and use the bricks to build durable walls of clay. Nobody had ever seen a man-made 'brick' before. So, through imagination and inspiration they were inventing brick-making and brick wall-building.

Nowadays there are university courses in brick building construction techniques and masonry. Nobody taught the settlers how to do it; there was no manual of masonry, no apprenticeship in brick-laying. They had to work it all out for themselves.

And one of their early successes would be unearthed – literally – in December 1984 when contractors digging the foundations for a planned new villa in Għajnsielem, beside what is now the main road from the harbour to Victoria, cut into and exposed a series of laid and resurfaced pre-historic floors of crushed stone… and with walls of clay 'bricks'.

*

Joe Attard Tabone, a local amateur archaeologist, spotted it and reported it to the National Museum of Archaeology at Valletta. Building work was stopped and archaeological excavation revealed two adjoining but distinct 'rooms': one small, almost square, about 2m across and the other, a larger oval space measuring about 8m by 5m with a raised rock foundation that also could have served as a surrounding wall seat. There was a roof-supporting pillar of clay bricks in the middle. Quite probably it would have been the first sloping roof in the Maltese islands.

This was the first full-scale excavation in Gozo for more than a century. A hard *torba* floor, repaired several times, revealed 'large quantities' of pottery, and also of imported (Sicilian) tools.

Torba meant layers of crushed limestone rock and chippings on a solid rubble base which was then repeatedly wetted down and pounded until, like cement, it was hard enough to polish. In the event of heavy usage or 'wear-and-tear' *torba* floors could easily be resurfaced – as had happened here on at least two occasions in the main structure and on four in the smaller one, suggesting regular hard use over a long period of time. Here, the *torba* was laid on a crushed stone filling about one foot (30cm) deep that provided insulation against cold and rising damp, and was surrounded by rock as the foundations for the walls.

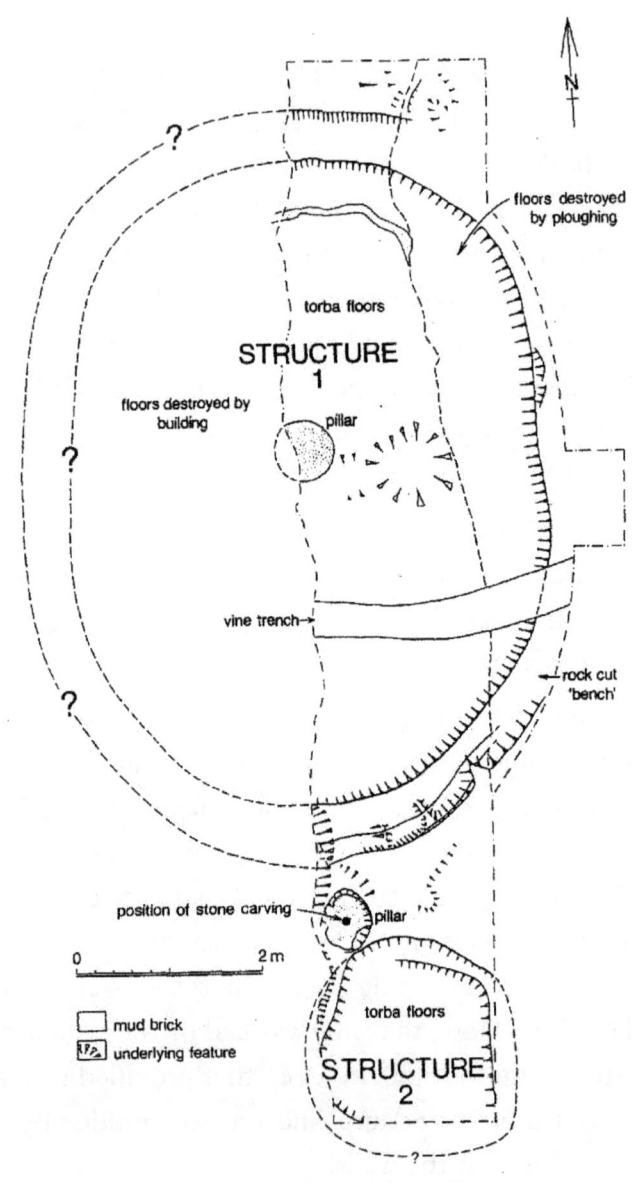

So it appears that these early settlers were both making bricks and inventing concrete, then erecting pillars to support their roofs, laying foundations and even damp-proofing to make their thoughtfully planned and carefully built homes – in spite of being constructed of 'mud'— both liveable and weather-proof, before (and possibly while) moving on to building in stone across the field. Long before any civilisations would be building 'temples', these people were building comfortably habitable houses.

*

This building, or the remains of it, was clearly part of a long-term settlement of more properties, much of it since lost to road-building, some to ploughing of the adjoining fields, some to the construction of neighbouring properties, but most importantly to the weather. 'Mud huts', even when inhabited, cannot expect a long life cycle against the natural elements of baking heat followed by occasional (typically four-day) bouts of torrential driving rain and fierce winds that occur even on an island known for its sunshine.

These two clay-brick rooms had been partially protected by a massive rubble field wall but also damaged by the digging of a vine trench and by the construction of neighbouring houses – whose foundations had not been reported.

Writing in *Gozo: The Roots of an Island*, Anthony Bonanno, professor of archaeology at Malta University, noted:

'The Għajnsielem discovery has proved to be very revealing with respect to the construction technique of domestic architecture.

It has shown that considerable care and attention was also lavished on the construction of houses but it has also confirmed that these houses were built of much flimsier and less durable material than the gigantic stones used for the temples, and this in itself accounts for their almost total disappearance from the Maltese archaeological record.'

The settlers had clearly had the same thought. If they wanted their buildings to endure, they needed to start building in stone.

They looked across their plateau and could see plenty of it, a few hundred yards away. And it was also closer to the main water supply…

The new adopted homeland, about 400 feet above sea level, had a view across the stunning vista of the channels to the north and west sides of Comino.

It was at a sufficient distance from the shore to be safe from any casual incursion by other tribes, but most importantly it had fresh water, running from underground streams that emerged in sufficiently combined strength to have created the deep fertile valley that runs, with stout bamboo stalks along its banks, down into the bay.

Geology

From the top of the next inland hill, the source of all the water (known as *Kenuna*, in Nadur, where a telegraph tower, built in 1848, now stands) they could see Sicily on a clear day, and even watch the eruptions of Etna from a safe distance – while occasionally getting flakes of its black volcanic ash in their hair and on their clothing.

The experienced farmers would have cleared some patches of *garigue* – the low-growing scrub of the Mediterranean that is the most common vegetation on the island – to examine the surface soil, and found it elbow deep in some places, but armpit deep in most of the rest.

It was deeper and more fertile than the soil a few miles away on Malta.

The strata show the geological history of the islands. You can see them by standing at sea level and looking at the sheer cliffs.

A fragmented crust of Upper Coralline, as its name suggests, is at the top and is formed from compressed coral, having risen 25-30 million years ago from a warm sea bed (or possibly having remained in the same position, as the sea level rose and receded, or perhaps having sunk and risen again). It is hard but brittle, often breaking up easily into stones that would come in handily for building.

Beneath the topsoil lies a very thin and inconsistent layer of 'greensand' (which is neither green nor sand and, apart from having derived from fossils and therefore possibly contributing slightly to the fertility of the soil, has no historical significance). Beneath that, the blue clay and then the basic coralline limestone of which the Maltese archipelago consists.

The Coralline rocks were what would determine the stone-built development of the islands and they came basically in two easily identifiable forms: soft and hard. The softer, yellow or honey-coloured, type (known to geologists as *Globigerina*), easy to cut, shape and to smooth, would come in handily for walls, both internal and external, and later for making sculptures. It is used in the same ways today.

As it has eroded slowly through many millennia, the grey Upper Coralline stone has produced what is known locally as *ħamrija* – reddish soil, exceptionally fertile because of its constituent corals, sea-urchins, molluscs and shells. Its enduring hardness made it useful for foundations and for paving slabs and cornerstones.

The blue clay was the second most important discovery. The farmers – or perhaps the farmers' wives (although there is no evidence of sexual differentiation in employment) – needed to make utensils for eating and for cooking: pots, bowls and cups with handles, certainly, and also something resembling spoons…

In fact they also invented a simple two-pronged clay fork, the broken pieces of which puzzled archaeologists until they found one complete and intact utensil – the fork was the handle of a spoon or ladle: a spoon with a fork at the other end. In the 1900s (AD) somebody would invent an eating tool for use by campers and adventurers called a 'spork' – a joint spoon and fork – and then patent it as an original invention.

The clay was also what created the water table, and thus was the provider of many useful springs in different parts of the islands (nowadays mostly identifiable by place names using *Għajn* as a prefix).

It would also come in handy for lining the cisterns or reservoirs the settlers chiselled out of the otherwise pervious rock to collect water during the rainy season and help see them through the weeks of predictable summer drought, although some streams carry water throughout almost the whole year.

*

Building in Stone

A few hundred yards away from the clay-brick dwellings, at most a five-minute walk over the plateau, was the main source of water for the settlement. And close to the water are the remains of more buildings, this time made of stone.

The water source and the water course, are still there, emanating from the spring at Kenuna, although the water nowadays runs underground to allow for the creation of a road – *triq fuq il-Għajn* ['road over the stream'] – which meets other, smaller, streams at *Fawwara* ['fast-flowing or overflowing'] and thence into *Wied il-Kbir* ['the great valley'], also known as 'the Bamboo Valley', which runs down to the sea.

Some of the buildings on the plateau, at least in outline, have survived the elements, but they stand unexcavated and unexplored by modern-day archaeologists. In fact, the site has been ignored to the extent that, like the development of the clay-brick settlement, a major road was built over and through it.

Its standing stones – proof of the lack of professional research is that archaeologists are still unsure about whether they involve two or three clusters of buildings – are listed as 'temples', which is a total misnomer because they have been identified as housing – 'cottages' and farm buildings.

And, echoing some settlements they may have seen – or even lived in – in Stentinello, at least one of the little group of buildings had a surrounding wall.

They would have the distinct advantage of creating their village of family and friends – all of whom could help each other with the erection of housing, with the clearing of pasture and the husbandry of their animal stock.

Confusingly, any building assumed to have been constructed during or close to the Maltese 'temple period' (3600 to 2500BC) is identified as a temple. It is an over-simplification for anything built by 'the temple builders' and, indeed, for anything built on the islands before the Bronze Age.

And it is here, then, that the people who would build Ġgantija built their homes, farmed their land, tended their animals, made their pottery, weaved their wool, spun their yarn and threshed their corn.

They planted barley, wheat and lentils and kept sheep, goats, pigs and cattle. (To give the as-yet unwritten *Sansuna* legend some credibility, they may also have had broad beans and kept bees.)

This was possibly, and perfectly probably, 2,000 years before anybody thought about the need for an actual 'temple' on Gozo, of any kind.

The archaeologists' rationalisation in favour of temples being, or having been, where megaliths are found includes the idea that the buildings with which they were associated were clearly important. After all (it is argued), a farmer could easily build his house with small rocks, much in the same way that he walled his fields; he would not go to the trouble of shifting such huge stones for anything as trivial as a house.

It may be so. On the other hand, a farmer might see a large stone in the ground close to where he wants to live and simply tilt it upright and use it as a corner... or a windbreak, and thereby the starting stone of his house.

The first stone masons may not have moved the giant rocks very far at all.

Perhaps interestingly, the Sicilians claim the honour of being the first home-builders in stone, so far as can be established by modern archaeology and excavation. Fair enough – these people were Sicilians, or at least of Sicilian descent. But their buildings were on 'Gozo'. And they would be the predecessors of the first 'Gozitans'.

It is also worth noting that nothing even remotely similar was ever built in Sicily.

Clay bricks were being used for building in Central Asia around this time, but in the rest of Europe house construction was still at the wattle-and-daub stage.

Gozo's race of 'temple builders' in stone was unique.

*

The First Village

To clear a plot of unforested land of topsoil stones, it is easy to imagine a farmer throwing them as far away as possible with all his might, and at the end of the day stacking them where they had landed, creating boundary walls.

These perimeters were not to mark ownership – there was no shortage of land: no need at this time to protect or argue about 'property'. In any case the landscape of the islands probably provided natural boundaries between adjoining settlements.

But the farm walls would serve as simple wind-breaks for newly planted crops, and would stabilise the top-soil in the event of heavy rain.

This would be an early example of what is now called 'dry-stone walling'. It was not an original creation, in Stentinello some farmers had identified and bordered their lands with ditches, while others had built stone walls. (But on Gozo it could perhaps explain why the fields and plots of land in modern times, inheriting those pre-historic boundary walls, are such irregular shapes.)

More imaginative than members of the tribe they had left behind, or simply 'evolving' from it, they would see the obvious potential beneficial effect of the walling and eventually apply it to domestic building, using the plentiful supply of sub-soil clay for in-filling the gaps. They were creating the first free-standing stone house-building known to man: thoughtfully laying flat stones at the base for foundation, and *torba* flooring, with loose stone carefully stacked above as walls, then in-filled with clay for added stability and for insulation from the elements, and in all likelihood, tree branches or rushes or bamboo from the valleys for roofing. Later, they would even use the abundant blue clay for decoratively 'plastering' their internal walls.

They used the soft limestone to build dwellings described by archaeologists as 'huts' or 'cottages': presumably because a 'house' would have more than one room inside its outer walls. And for security from the weather and from the (unlikely) possibility of incursion, they built a perimeter wall of the harder grey and heavy coralline limestone in a rough circle to encompass and secure their cluster of homes of family and friends.

The hard coralline was difficult to carve or to shape, but could be split along its often-visible fissures by chiselling with flint, then hammering dry wooden wedges into it, and soaking them with water to make them expand. Perhaps they also used fire to split them with heat. Either technique would often produce flat slabs that could be used for flooring, as paving slabs. Nobody of whom they were aware had ever done anything like it before.

The remains of the arc of one circular outer stone wall at *L-Imrejżbiet* – across the field from the 'mud-hut' site – are clearly visible to this day. This appears to be the eastern limit of a smallish (although probably, at the time of building, and to its earliest inhabitants, a fairly large) village community. The site – or what could be seen of it – was fully described more than 100 years ago by Albert Mayr (1868-1924), a Bavarian archaeologist and historian who had developed an interest in the prehistoric and pre-Christian history of Malta and Gozo – even before he had set foot on the islands.

Parts of the stone circular wall at L-Imrejżbiet, limits of Għajnsielem. Behind is a row of modern houses where development was halted by the discovery of a building in clay brick. An aerial view gives a better impression of the circular shape and its limitation of a ploughed field.

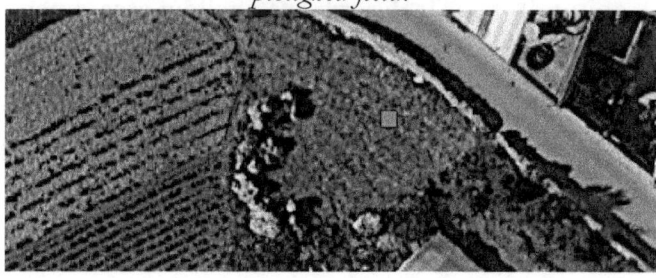

His first visit to Malta was in 1897. On Gozo he reported the remains of what he identified as a fortified settlement 'in the wide plain extending inward from the bay of *Mjiar*':

> 'About 750 yards north-west of the village of *Ghajnsielem* there is a plateau-like elevation of the ground which extends for a length of 500 paces and with a width of about 100 paces...
>
> 'This elevation attains heights from 6 feet to 13 feet and is sharply delimited on the north where the rock of which it consists breaks off abruptly. The ruins... are situated on the eastern side of this eminence near a field known as *tal-Kaghan* [Tal-Qighan] ...
>
> 'The corner of another ancient wall still remains here of which one side can be traced for a distance of about 45 feet. The modern field wall which forms the continuation northwards also contains ancient stones for the distance of another 32 feet. The wall extending towards the west and forming the other side of the angle is in a bad state of preservation and, with a breach in it, can be traced for a length of about 40 feet. It describes a shallow area, open to the south.'

He reported that the walls were composed of rough blocks or slabs. The largest stones were two vertical slabs marking a corner of the site. These measured about two metres in width and three metres in height:

> 'The form of this corner and the shallow are described by the wall extending westwards, *are strongly reminiscent of the façades of extant temple buildings*, and the author feels no doubt but that these remains form part of the anterior side and of the enclosure wall of a similar construction. Within the ancient walls and the modern layers of stones forming the continuation there is a field about 70 paces long and half as wide. The present surface is strikingly high and it is quite possible that important ruins of the buildings which once stood here may be buried in this field.'

Mayr described the remains as being 'carelessly built, of rather small material' that 'can only have been the sub-structures of cottages or houses':

(Not, then, of 'temples.)

> 'Their upper parts may have consisted of earth or clay and the roofing, which on account of the narrowness of the compartments could have offered no difficulty, was perhaps composed of faggots bound together and covered with earth and clay…'

He was, therefore, looking at homes, not at places of worship. The word 'temple', when used to describe any work of the temple-building peoples, again becomes distracting.

Mayr documented sites, took photographs and drew his own ground-plans. He considered his attempted documentation incomplete since he had to leave 'many gaps that were impossible to fill'.

In 1901 he complained about the lack of protection and the wilful destruction of monuments. He criticised the insufficient recording systems of local museums, which made it impossible to trace the provenance of finds.

Perhaps because he was writing in German, about Mediterranean islands that then formed a British colony, or maybe because he challenged the legendary claims of early Christianity in Malta as likely medieval fabrications (or, more politely, simply 'wrong conclusions'), which would not have endeared him to local society, much of his work has been overlooked.

He was not the first explorer to discover, and to report on, evidence of pre-historic life at *'tal-Kaghan'*.

Antonio Annetto had probably been the first, in 1884, to find, and to record, the presence of the sites and of a tomb cave in the area.

Caruana, who was Malta's librarian (1880–1896) and Director of Education (1887–1896) was not an archaeologist but an interested, enthusiastic and dedicated amateur. He thought the buildings *included* 'a temple'. He perhaps meant only a building dating from 'the Temple Period' – one of the structures that Mayr said were cottages or houses.

Caruana was interested in the caves. He wrote of one of

them: 'unfortunately… that interesting tomb had already been rifled… and cleared of the greater part of its contents, and the cave itself destroyed to give way to the construction of a public road.'

He continued:

> 'The type of this tomb could not, consequently, be determined by inspection. Besides, no indications of the position of the skulls and bones were obtained and no notes of other particulars with regard to the interments found in it were furnished. From the topographical knowledge of the place, however… and the nature and quantity of relics obtained, I feel warranted to conclude that it was an isolated tomb, or a family tomb, in which no less than five individuals were interred, unconnected with any cluster of tombs.
>
> 'The situation of this Tomb Cave … is in the extensive heath of sandstone formation, outside the recent village of Ghain Sielem, on the SE slope of the denuded southern tip of the island, towards the sea of Migiarr… This cave penetrated 5ft inside the rock, beneath the level ground of the road, where it had a circular opening and extended over 8ft longitudinally.'

Caruana discovered other caves at *Fawwara*. He wrote:

> 'Often, they penetrate twelve or more feet inside the

rock, appearing like an antechamber, communicating with inner and smaller caves through arched and low apertures, nearly at the same ground level of the exterior cave, exhibiting the cellular arrangement of a family tomb. The illustration of the tomb at Kasam-el-Fauura shows one of these instances…'

[*Kasam* means 'area of'; *Fauura* is the writer's spelling of Fawwara, where all the rivulets from the Kenuna hill combine to create *Wied il-Kbir* (the 'great valley') of Għajnsielem.

The main water course was the Simirat Valley, long since piped and paved to become 'the road over the stream'.

Inside the caves he found human skulls and partial skeletons, and pottery – jugs, a flask, a cup, plates and a jar. He reckoned that such caves could 'safely be assigned an age somewhat beyond 3,000 years'.

Those caves are now hidden by another 'road over the stream' – by the houses on either side of Fawwara-street, between the fountain and the valley.

Perhaps stating the obvious, Caruana noted that tomb caves were 'invariably found in the proximity of old centres of habitation'. However, there was going to be a limit to the number of dead that could be integrated into the fabric of a village…

Mayr and Caruana were the first to recognise and to date the settlement as originating further back than the previously assumed pre-Roman and Phoenician-Carthaginian period of occupation, which was approximately 750BC to 218BC, when the Romans took over the Maltese islands as part of their defence of Sicily.

*

In 1988, after examining the clay brick end of the development, Professor Caroline Malone (Queens University Belfast) wrote:

> 'The discovery of these remains provokes some questions about the survival of domestic structures on the Maltese Islands. Since the discovery of the Għajnsielem Road huts, other possible settlements have been located in buildings sites and by very preliminary surface field survey.
>
> 'Until these discoveries, archaeologists on Malta had failed to prospect for buried, protected or otherwise undisturbed sites where delicate structures might survive. In the current climate of major urban development of the islands, an integrated rescue and research project is required to record this threatened information.'

So after a century of 'modern' archaeology, the more recent half of it aided by scientific dating, we still have sites on Malta and Gozo that are undiscovered, and sites that are known about, but which remain unexcavated and examined.

It seems that 'amateurs' have been able to find easily, or by chance, what the professionals haven't been able to find, or haven't bothered to look for.

The *Tal-Qigħan* section of this early village was only part – perhaps two-thirds – of the stone-built settlement that at some stage in its history became known as *L-Imrejżbiet*. The arc-wall section was separated from the rest and overbuilt by the (Xewkija to Qala) road referred to by Caruana.

Interestingly, and perhaps importantly, a *qigħan* in Arabic-Maltese is a threshing floor – a flat stone paved area, usually circular, used for processing cereals.

Sheaves of corn would be opened up and the stalks spread across the *qigħan* and then farmers would crunch it with their feet or bash it with stones to tear the ears of corn from the stalks and loosen the grain itself from the husks.

Stone spheres, about the size of a grapefruit, have been identified by some archaeologists as most likely having been used for sling-shots.

But, as there were no animals to hunt, and no known predators, nor any enemies and no other form of weaponry, it might be that they were used for grinding cereals by hand. After this 'threshing' process, the broken stalks and grain were collected and then thrown up into the air. The chaff would be blown away by the wind (suggesting that the floor itself would be in the open air).

Neolithic threshing tools

The short, torn straw would fall some distance away; while the heavier grain would fall at the farmer's feet.

This was literally 'sorting the wheat from the chaff'. The grain could then be further sorted by hand.

If this was the working space, the other site was the residential area and there may have been no actual 'temple' – no place of 'worship' – within the settlement.

It is also perhaps noteworthy, if only in passing, that the structure of the surviving prehistoric *Kordin* remains near Malta's Grand Harbour include a 2.7m flooring slab of Coralline limestone that must have been dragged for more than a kilometre from the nearest visible formation of that form of rock and which archaeologists have deduced was most probably imported to be used for threshing cereal crops.

Nevertheless, that site, which includes an extensive village area behind it, is also described as a 'temple'. And archaeologists are still wondering about the implications of a temple with a threshing stone within it.

*

The People

It is more than likely that several generations, even several centuries, passed between the first steps on shore and the creation of a civilised industrial-agricultural development of the stone *L-Imrejżbiet* housing settlement. In fact 5600BC seems to the best actual 'guesstimate' for the arrival of the first visitors.

To put this into a context of historical importance, building is said to have started on Stonehenge in 3100BC; – 500 years later than at Ġgantija. The oldest Pyramid was built around 2600BC, about 1,000 years more recently. Interestingly, all three of these original buildings were also the first constructions in dressed (shaped and smoothed) stone.

Stonehenge (above); Ġgantija (below)

Oddly, Ġgantija, the oldest, seems to be the least famous.

On a wider Mediterranean and religious dateline, the Biblical *Book of Exodus* – a point of reference for Jews, Christians and Muslims – although written a long time afterwards, describes events involving Moses and probably Ramesses the Second (or Rameses The Great), who was pharaoh of Egypt around 1200BC.

*

So, what can be deduced about this tribe of people who would be the first in Europe to build groups of houses in stone?

That they were farmers is obvious – for only farmers would have been aware of this far-off island, and able to subsist once they had arrived.

The days of the hunter-gatherer were over: there was nothing on Gozo or Malta to hunt and little to gather.

The settlers were certainly adventurous. They were intelligent enough to learn to sail and to navigate. They were industrious – they couldn't have survived, otherwise. They were traders – without doubt bartering their individual style of pottery and surplus foodstuffs to buy tools from Sicily.

They would develop for themselves, and would share, at least a primitive understanding of both architecture and construction. And, as would later emerge, they were artistic.

It is however important to remember that there was no

external source to teach these vital skills. Anything they didn't know on their departure from Sicily they had to learn for themselves as they went along.

Since they were going to build Ġgantija they were also obviously strong. Skeletal remains – the ones that proved they were not giants – show an exceptionally healthy population for the period with no signs of malnutrition and an absence of tooth decay. There was even a noticeable absence of bone fractures, suggesting that they worked relatively safely.

The skeletal evidence actually indicates that the people, and their domesticated animals, became slightly smaller as they evolved. With no more roaming for their survival they needed to be less 'rugged' in their build. Their working routines, although still extremely hard, became relatively static and regularised, and their physique adapted to it.

A settled environment anchored to house and village and, consequently, domesticity, no doubt created an increase in the rate of human reproduction, and, with housing, a tendency towards monogamy which had not necessarily been part of their previous culture.

A 'nuclear household', now solidly stationary, would typically consist of three generations: one set of grandparents, husband and wife and two to four surviving children (for the rate of child mortality was between 40 and 50 per cent). The stronger family members (probably, but not necessarily exclusively, the men) would handle the building work, digging, hoeing and harrowing, and herding and eventually slaughtering the livestock, while the weaker would be tasked with baking, sowing, tending the vegetable plot, sowing seeds (and bird-scaring), cooking, milking... and pottery.

If they had started to 'harvest' salt, that would have been another light job, and maybe useful for trade.

Even without any structure of division of labour by gender, regular and uncontrolled human pregnancies, followed by nursing, reduced female mobility and kept the women closer to home. It is more than likely that the houses and the garden plots around them became 'the woman's place', while the men were in sometimes distant fields.

An increase in family members meant more hands that were available for work, but more mouths to feed. Sufficiency was not the same as efficiency: families needed to overproduce their food supply, to protect against future bad harvests, against droughts and flooding... and to provide a surplus of something that they could trade.

At least in the early years cooking and eating would be done outdoors. It is therefore likely that it would have been a communal practice, involving more than one family – perhaps, at least while it was small, the entire community.

This would take place in a central area that was usually paved or cobbled... to avoid mud, maybe, or perhaps to mark a village 'centre'.

All sorts of other activities took place there: the knapping (shaping) of stone tools, firing pottery, the processing of skins, teaching of skills and generally just sitting and talking to each other.

Indoors was for sleeping and shelter... outdoors was for living.

*

The Festa

With cows, sheep and pigs having a productive life of eight to ten years, and being more valuable on the hoof than in the larder, meat-eating could well have been an occasion for a village feast.

After all, what else does the 'nuclear family' do with 500lbs (say 225kg) of edible meat from a recently slaughtered cow? It is far more than a family of around ten people – half of whom would be children—could consume while it was fresh. There was no form of refrigeration. It might be feasible to 'dry' or to smoke or salt some of it. But the obvious solution would be to eat it, and to invite the neighbours round to share it, rather than to let it rot.

And there you have a village *festa*.

With a bit of forethought animals could be slaughtered to coincide with a celebration: of a betrothal or consummation, or of childbirth. The beast's owner would nominate the occasion and announce a meat feast.

Historians who are desperate to find religiosity in the habits of prehistoric Gozitans might interpret such celebrations as 'rituals'. The neighbours, whose main diet was based on cereals and eating the equivalent of about a kilo of bread or porridge a day (the evidence is in the teeth), were not likely to refuse the invitation.

While the consumption of lamb or goats might have been a common experience inside families, the slaughter of a cow and the meat on it created an excuse for a social occasion.

It therefore seems possible, and highly probable, that the eating of beef would take place only in, and as part of, a large and neighbourly event.

From that custom would discretely emerge a sort of casual hierarchy – the family with the most (or the best) food gradually but naturally assuming a position of precedence. Food-stock and skills (and, perhaps, signs of intelligence) were the only ways of calculating 'wealth' and prestige.

Well, perhaps not the only ways. For scheduling a party to convert a quarter of a ton of rapidly deteriorating meat into a celebration surreptitiously puts the cow owner in charge of local festivities (and maybe of 'rituals'), and automatically gives him some control over the seasonal social timetable.

It puts the neighbours who eat his food under an obligation, and into his debt. (It also gives him the right to share in the meat-eating of other families, in the future.)

Assuming that they followed the Neolithic Sicilian-Italian pattern, the 'richest' family might have kept a herd of around 30 cattle with about twice as many sheep and goats. (Thirty cows seems to be a number economically sufficient to form minimum protection against drought, disease, and fluctuations in fertility.)

If that size of smallholding, also with pigs foraging around the woodland and occasionally needing rounding up and checking, was too big for one family to manage alone, there was always the possibility of hiring labour in exchange for food or goods.

And with that power of ownership and perhaps also of employment would come – again, possibly discretely – the mantle of perceived local power and leadership.

The emergence of community leaders is unattested but likely as a matter of common sense. Somebody with both wealth and wisdom would automatically fulfil that role as, in animal terms, 'leader of the pack'. It is also a natural human practice.

It may have been the oldest member of a village who was considered to be the wisest, based on the notion of greatest experience. In which case they were creating a system of the seniority of 'elders', who, in those days, could have been anybody over forty.

Although there is little evidence of privilege visible in forms of burial, there are occasional instances of special treatment in that some of the bodies were accompanied by, for example, miniature axes, or by shell jewellery, while others were not.

What is clear is that all their dead were treated with considerable respect.

*

The 'Temple Builders'

So much for the first inhabitants of Malta… history's first 'Gozitans'… That is how the people of Għajnsielem and of Santa Verna (and maybe in other places in Gozo as yet undiscovered) would have lived.

Little is known about Santa Verna, other than that it had mud huts and a burial cave.

But there can, or should, be no doubt about it – those people living in what's now called Għajnsielem were among the masons who built the 'Ġgantija temple' complex.

Referring to the Mġarr road section of the settlement, Professor Bonanno told this writer that the site was 'where the temple builders lived'.

Professor Malone, working on the clay-brick buildings with Dr Simon Stoddart (Magdalene College, Cambridge) and Dr David Trump, curator at the National Museum of Archaeology, Malta, wrote:

> 'The most impressive aspect of the two small structures on Gozo is the obvious care and attention lavished on their construction. It should come as no surprise that *the people who were responsible for erecting the Maltese temples* were equally capable of building comfortable well designed 'houses'.

'However, outside the east Mediterranean, there are no examples of similarly well-built and designed buildings in the early 3rd millennium BC in Western Europe. Contemporary sites on Sicily have produced only scant traces of settlement structures.'

This is not to say that other local communities didn't contribute to the 'temple'-building. They obviously did, because the construction plainly required an enormous workforce.

The people of Taċ-Ċawla for example, whose pottery seems to have shown a particularly artistic ability (and who at some stage also built in stones), may have designed Ġgantija – we don't know who the architect was.

But the folk with the obvious building experience were living at *L-Imrejżbiet* and *Tal-Qigħan*. And Mayr had remarked on their development being 'strongly reminiscent of the façades of extant temple buildings' (by which, presumably, he meant the nearest – Ġgantija).

However, the Bavarian archaeologist almost certainly had things the wrong way round...

It was, of course, the temples that were 'strongly reminiscent' of the Għajnsielem buildings, either side of the Qala road, which were clearly earlier examples of this early people's stone-building ability.

And since the settlers lived there, in houses built of stone, and since the builders were there a long time – several hundred years – before construction started on any 'temples' it stands to reason that these sites, and not Ġgantija, could possibly (if excavated and examined) lay claim to being *'the earliest surviving examples of free-standing stone-built structures in the world'.*

That the builders made their own homes first, and organised their shelter and food sources before embarking on the construction of a gigantic monument, seems to be the most logical way of doing things.

*

Stone-carved standing figure of pre-historic man (or woman?) found at Hagar Qim.
(About 50cm tall).

*

Trading

The evolution of the simplest economy for their lifestyle as an actual civilised, organised community must have required a whole series of fairly regular supply and trading trips between Sicily and Gozo.

Producing only sufficient for their own needs – simple subsistence farming (and pottery-making) – would have been economically inefficient: it was vital to generate a surplus – of wool, sheepskin and leather hides, perhaps of finished clothing, and, once manufacture got into full flow, of their own design of pottery, too – to exchange for goods, especially chiselling and cutting implements, back home on Sicily.

They would have needed to replace their tools as they wore out and occasionally to acquire a new bull and male pig to avoid in-breeding and to refresh their herd.

There was no 'money' [coinage would be invented in Lydia, now Turkey, around 600BC], so all dealings relied on a system of exchange: 'I will feed your family if you help build my house'… 'I have a surplus of milk but a shortage of vegetables…'

International trading (between Sicily and Gozo or even Gozo to Malta) was conducted on the basis of an exchange of 'gifts'. The would-be 'purchaser' made a present of something that he knew or hoped that the 'seller' wanted. The 'seller' would then return the compliment by offering something that (in order not to lose face) would be at least equal in value, to him, as his response to the gift he had just received.

The Gozitan farmers could possibly refresh their herds by exchanges among the new breeds being imported to the island (and fairly easily with their counterparts on Malta) but in order to trade with Sicily they probably preferred to take more portable material. They could have taken preserved meat, or salt, wool, woven clothing, leather hides, and maybe their own style of clay-cast cooking pots to exchange for (most importantly) flint and obsidian.

In order to do this they would, of course, need to sail back. Maintaining at least one of their vessels in good condition for the homeward journey could have been a full-time job for one or more people. How would these early shipwrights be encouraged and rewarded? With food, shelter, clothing, tools, no doubt: there was nothing else to offer.

[Despite the absence of evidence, it seems difficult to imagine even a small population on Malta and Gozo existing without supplementing their diet with fish. The people who made the crossing from Sicily had acquired both boat building and boat handling skills. Some of them must have taken to it, perhaps in preference to agriculture. There is every reason to assume the existence of a small 'fishing fleet'. And these people would have been the ones best able to keep the boats in sufficiently good order to make the long crossing to Sicily.]

Then they needed to plan the voyage at a time when they would have the wind behind them. But this required relying on the dreaded sand-carrying Sirocco, which could come across the islands at hurricane force, but maybe in only short bursts. Most common in autumn and spring, the wind speed would normally peak in March and in November and then develop into red rain, coloured by the sand.

It was not going to be a comfortable journey, but somebody had to do it and that would probably be the head of the family that had items to trade and who needed goods that could be acquired only on Sicily. He would have to schedule the voyage when he could be spared from his fields for however long the return journey would take.

And a genuinely successful trading exercise – not, certainly, embarked upon except through absolute necessity – might well provide an excuse, after sailing back and finding home, for another *festa*. Perhaps they brought back new Sicilian designs of pottery that they could improve, or copy, and thus maintain the evolution of ceramics on which modern archaeologists would become so dependent.

Trading was then, as ever, a question of supply and demand. What does one person have a surplus of, when the other has a shortage? Bring the two together and you have trade.

Creating the community

The next chapter of the Ġgantija story requires a great deal of imagination and assumption while trying to remain within the bounds of possibility, logic and likelihood.

We know that there was pottery making at Santa Luċija and wall-building at Taċ-Ċawla and il-Mixta. We know that there was stone building and agricultural industry at L-Imrejżbiet and Tal-Qigħan in Għajnsielem. Professor Malone has reported other possible settlements 'located in building sites and by very preliminary surface field survey'. So we can safely assume that, in the 2,000 or so years since the first landing of Man on the island, it now comprised a number of settled communities.

In time, they must have found each other. Perhaps they met occasionally, and even helped each other, in times of drought or of flash floods when crops might be destroyed or livestock endangered in some areas, while not in others, even on a very small island.

They were peaceable, certainly (no prehistoric weapons of any kind have been found on the island). Man is, after all, firstly a social animal.

It is likely that some sort of kinship developed quickly between the separate small communities for, just as they were probably aware of the need to avoid inbreeding of cattle and sheep, they must have had at least some notion of the need for 'fresh blood' in human procreation.

It is still, nowadays, not unusual for cousins to marry in Malta, and marriages 'within the village' are not uncommon. A modern father might still ask his son, who announces his intention to marry a girl from a different parish: 'What's wrong with her? Why don't the boys in her own village want her?' It astonishes non-Maltese to learn how frequently immigrants in places like Australia manage to meet and to marry people whose family comes from their own village back home.

So, on a remote island like Gozo, there would soon have been quite literally a familiarity between the different small communities, doubtless sharing problems, and sharing knowledge. They would also have developed a common method of communication (language), of traditions and maybe of superstitions, and of culture – in this sense including both artistic and behavioural.

There would have been an outstanding common interest… in simply surviving.

None of this should imply that prehistoric life was in any way idyllic. Farming is an industry in which the solution to a problem is often another problem.

They may have been unaware of the advantages of crop rotation – alternating vegetables in different plots that would absorb different ground nutrients. But as farmers they would have learnt by experience of the need to leave land to lie fallow and recover fertility, and would have created more fresh space by gradually depleting the island's natural woodland. This, in turn, would have increased the rate of natural soil erosion.

Intensive farming also degrades the fertility of the soil and cyclical use of different fields requires logistics. The need for grassland for grazing is year-round, but sheep will chew it down to ground level while goats will gnaw at... almost anything.

While it may not have been necessary to separate the sheep from the goats (something that forensic archaeologists find difficult to do when examining skeletal remains); it was preferable for them to be separated from the cattle. And both to be separated from the pigs. They all had to be kept out of the vegetable garden.

They required different pastures, and they naturally fertilized the patch in which they lived. Then the farmer needed to rotate the stock on an annual basis among all the fields within his freely acquired agricultural domain.

Neolithic Man was no longer nomadic. He was king of his own realm. But an island is, by definition, finite in area. Even with the addition of Malta, close by, Gozo had only so much land to work, and to work on.

Since Man was now static, it was the land around him that had to change in order to remain useful. It all required planning, and hard work. (And this was before the additional hard labour that would come with 'temple' building.)

Furthermore, in a relatively new isolated community, or group of communities, there were also the constant fears of bad luck from the capricious weather; of bad harvests that threatened at least temporary famine; the possibility of illness or disease, both animal and human; the potential dangers of inbreeding (again, both animal and human); the issues created by a frequently changing population that needed to be fed.

Add to this the primitive harsh living conditions and the incessant need for intensive labour and it may be difficult to understand how an apparently contented population could survive over so many centuries without cooperation and collaboration while continuing to toil and reproduce and to maintain and develop its culture of art and architecture for so many centuries.

For this they certainly did. The evidence is still there for us to wonder at.

*

Council Meeting

There is a saying that if two Englishmen were cast away on a deserted island, the first thing they would do is to form a club… three or more and they would form a committee. (Other nationalities may behave in the same way.)

Perhaps the Sican-Sicilians behaved similarly.

Maybe, like the legendary giant women with *Il-Ġemgħa tal-Ġganti* they created a 'council', perhaps of the 'elders' or obvious leaders of each community. Democracy, some form of voting, was yet to be invented, but it is a natural trait to accept leadership, even casually; we see it with bulls, stags, dogs and with people: the natural leaders of the pack emerge quite quickly, one way or another.

The villages would, after all, have common problems, concerns, or needs – not least, for example, in trading, in sending one boat to Sicily once or twice a year, instead of sending several.

Some farmsteads would have shortages when others might have a surplus. Some might need to borrow (or to hire?) additional manpower at certain times of the year. The form of meeting in which this sort of problem could be raised and aired might well have involved including their counterparts across the channel on Malta.

But one of the local matters that would have to be faced at some stage would be what the different groups or communities could do with the bodies of their dead family members on a small island like Gozo.

Caruana, the happy amateur, noted that he had discovered a number of family tombs in caves, sometimes extended by having been chiselled further into the rock. Different families apparently occupied separate tomb-caves. He had noticed five 'family members' in one of them. In the small area of Tal-Qigħan he had found a few similar examples.

And his discovery that the remains were accompanied by items like jugs, flasks and cups surely suggests some kind of death ritual, in even the earliest settlements. We might guess that the dead were being provided for in their journey into the unknown world beyond.

There seems to be no other logical explanation for it.

From the histories of other ancient civilisations, it would appear that reverence of their ancestors was a perfectly natural human phenomenon in different communities in different isolated parts of the world.

Many peoples believed in a life continuing, in some form, after death, where the point of death was the start of a journey towards some form of afterlife. So they placed their precious possessions (and sometimes food for the journey) alongside them. Where possible, deceased family members were interred together.

It was one way of handling the obvious question after 'Where do we come from?'… 'Where do we go next?'

So the corpses were cared for.

In the 1940s Monsignor Paolo Buttigieg, another enthusiastic amateur archaeologist, taking a sabbatical on Gozo from his job as chancellor of the Curia in Malta, discovered even more caves at Tal-Qigħan. There were skeletons inside them caringly separated by fine soil.

The entrances to these 'tomb caves' were sealed by huge stones, a practice that the Bible tells us was still common at the time of Christ.

This system of disposal of a family's loved ones may well have sufficed when communities were small. But as populations increased, so would the number of corpses. Any village, especially one with walls around it – even one with its own caves in the vicinity – could cater for only a limited number.

Alternative sites had to be found. And this might well have been an important item on the agenda for an early 'council meeting'.

If there were to be a communal burial place, suitable for all the island's dead, it would ideally be relatively equidistant for all the villages. It would already have caves – for the early settlers had not realised that digging graves in the soil (where they could find sufficient depth of it) and burying wrapped corpses would have been easier.

(Or maybe soil was too precious to spoil.)

While the premise of a communal meeting with decisions being taken by a 'council' of village elders is obviously pure conjecture, the archaeological evidence is undoubtedly proof that something very similar must have happened.

It would appear that land at Santa Verna in Xagħra, where pioneer settlers had already started farming on a beautiful stretch of fertile land and – possibly as early as 5000BC – had created a small community of clay or clay-brick housing, was chosen as the location. It was to become a burial place for a community far bigger than Santa Verna's alone.

Perhaps, having no access to a map of the island (nor any need for one) they saw this place as being near enough to the centre of the island – sufficiently close and equally accessible to families from all the settlements.

In 2017 building permission for the nearby fields – on a long plateau with a spring beneath it, about 140m above sea level, and roughly half way between the imposing 'Citadel hill' and the attractive bay at Ramla il-Ħamra – was denied to a potential developer, on the grounds that the fields were 'packed with Neolithic skeletons'.

Apart from three megaliths, the tallest being 3m high, little remains of the site today, and it has not been fully examined, although there is some visible evidence of a trefoil ['clover-leaf'] outline on the topsoil, which might replicate the shape of the oval tomb caves beneath it. In which case it could explain the origin of that unusual design for the start of Ġgantija and the other 'temple' sites throughout the archipelago that generally recreated its distinctive outline.

Following Santa Verna, or perhaps concurrent with it, another cave structure was opened a few hundred yards away at what would become known as the Xagħra Circle.

It is actually a circle – a walled enclosure, although the wall itself seems to have come from much older megalithic structures – and there was already a subterranean cave system in the soft stone. The extended construction suggests to some that burials were made in cave tombs around a central area that may have been intended for a final funerary 'ritual', although this may be doubtful because the Circle was regularly short of space and in need of extension.

Excavations within it have uncovered not just bones but also an extraordinary number of man-made sculpted objects – one depicting 'twins', and a cache of stick figures, among them.

Importantly, the objects could be studied by architects in context, in relation to each other, to the buried individuals they accompanied, and to the structures that enclosed them.

Many Maltese students learnt archaeology first-hand through their participation in the digs on this site.

Bodies found in this deeply excavated *hypogeum* [the word translates literally as 'underground'] inside a system of natural caves on a hilltop, have been dated from 4100BC…

that is 500 years before work started on construction of the Ġgantija project, but nearly 1,000 years after it has been presumed that Santa Verna was first inhabited.

According to Dr David Trump,

> 'the main purpose of this [Xagħra Circle] site was clearly for burial, making it a veritable necropolis. Study of the bones, still continuing, has given a tally so far of at least 800 individuals.'

That was in 2004AD.

*

Once established, the tombs seem generally to have followed the village pattern: where possible keeping family members together and occasionally – but not necessarily always – providing some form of comfort, perhaps also items of jewellery worn during their lifetimes, to accompany them during their journey into the unknown. If these pendants or tokens, mainly pierced bones or shells, had a superstitious benefit during lifetime, it must have been assumed that the 'charm' would survive in the afterlife.

At a later stage the bodies would often be liberally sprinkled or painted with red ochre – presumably to represent blood and life. The paint was an oxide of iron that was not found naturally in Malta or Gozo. It was another material that had to be traded and imported from Sicily, probably originally sourced from the area around Agrigento.

It doesn't require a great leap of imagination to speculate that since seeds, gathered from plants at the end of their natural life cycle, would regenerate in a new life form if buried, a similar thing might happen with people.

The siting of a first communal burial site may have been the first important island-wide decision that the 'elders' (if such a council existed) would have needed to take. But there was more to come.

*

At some, probably later, stage in the island's pre-history, somebody suggested that they needed to combine all their efforts and build a gigantic structure – the one that would eventually be called Ġgantija.

We can make that assumption on the basis that it was certainly too big a project for one settlement to handle alone: a single community would not have been able to afford the manpower or the time away from its fields.

But what was the purpose of the building that this visionary had in mind? What was he (or she) suggesting? What did the combined community agree that it needed so desperately, on such a grand scale?

Unless the self-importance of 'community leaders' has changed greatly over the intervening millennia, they might have fancied a parliament building, a council chamber in which they could all meet importantly and in comfort in all weathers. But if there were only one or two representatives of each 'village' they could all have sat comfortably around the walls of the larger clay-brick room in Għajnsielem.

Perhaps the instigator suggested a community centre, where the entire population of the island could meet – although the internal size and shape of the accepted design indicates that this would not have been the case.

Or suppose it was suggested as a common holding space where each community could store its produce, and even trade or exchange it with others. Each village or farm could have had one of several 'leaves' of a clover pattern for storage, with a table at the back on which it could display its finest or superfluous goods. Yet that seems unlikely, because the original plan envisaged only three recesses.

We can, however, safely assume that at some stage – possibly having reached agreement by consensus that there was indeed a need to construct a great building for Gozo – somebody drew or etched an outline of the construction with a stone or stick.

Whichever way the original plan was worked out, it was surely the brainchild of an individual, rather than of a committee.

We don't know, and will probably never know with any degree of certainty, what inspired this uniquely designed architectural wonder, or who had the original inspiration.

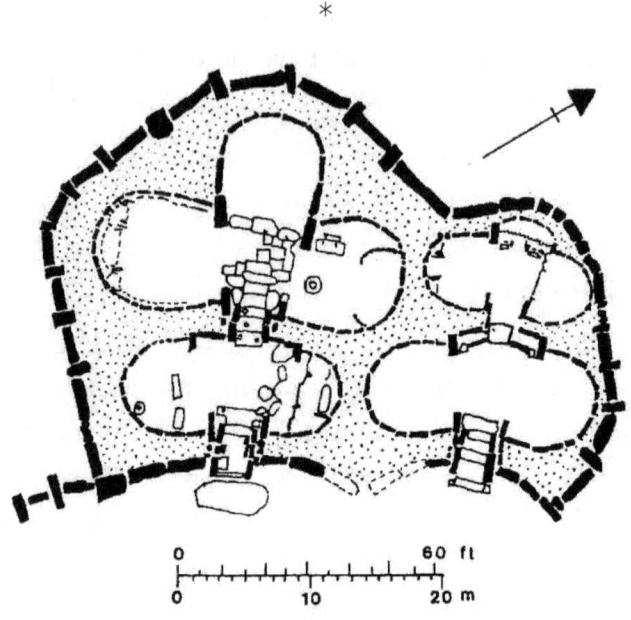

If one accepts the fairly reasonable idea that these people were preoccupied with the idea of 'fertility' – human, animal and agricultural – it is not too difficult to accept the suggestion that the artist intended his original clover-leaf or trefoil design to depict the head and breasts of a woman.

A less romantic theory is that, underground burials being commonplace, with caves chiselled out in ovals, the idea was simply to replicate the burial chambers – tall 'caves' built above ground level – as an intermediate resting place.

(It is otherwise difficult to imagine what might have inspired such an unusual blueprint. 'Let's build a massive temple with three, then five, then ten, linked altars' might appear to have been an unlikely proposition...)

Whoever it was, the visionary was a great architect and a master builder with a fantastic imagination who could see the finished building in his (or her) mind. Someone who knew the types of stone available – hard rock on the outer walls to protect against the prevailing and erosive wind and softer stone used for walls internally. And then a rubble, *torba* or paved court at the front of the building.

All of this would require the movement of large lumps of both hard and soft rocks. They had to be sourced, they needed to be manoeuvred to the site, and they had to be erected according to a plan.

The Great Architect knew that it could be done.

Other members of the community (most likely one decision needing to be taken by consensus, rather than by unanimity, because it was going to be closer and more accessible to some communities than to others) chose the site.

Would it have been accepted immediately? Were there alternative suggestions? All we know is that a decision was made that it was necessary and also about what it would look like. And then agreement was reached about where to build it. That was going to be between the cave tombs of Santa Verna and the Xagħra Circle.

Building is believed to have started around 3600BC. For all we know, the arguments about the need for it, and about the design of it, and then the positioning of it could have taken hundreds of years, perhaps a hundred generations.

That Neolithic man could build in stone was not in doubt. There may have been other communities dwelling in caves, or even in stone, but on the edge of what is now Għajnsielem, we know that they had built houses of stone, and that at *Taċ-Ċawla* (limits of Victoria) and at *il-Mixta* (outside San Lorenz) they had at least one stone wall each. So there were stone-masons. And maybe even early architects, since Mayr noticed elements of what he saw as 'design' in the houses on the Għajnsielem site that were reflected in Ġgantija.

*

What God?

Somebody, at some much later point in time, looked at Ġgantija and decided that it had been built as a temple, and so it became known as the Ġgantija Temple, and although the word 'temple' remains optional in this specific context, the epoch during which it was built (approximately 3600-2500BC) started being, and is still, referred to as the Temple Period, and all the inhabitants of the Maltese islands are known as the Temple Builders – even those who never lifted a stone except to clear a field.

But a temple (*Oxford English* dictionaries) is 'a building devoted to the worship of a god or gods'.

If the settlers of Gozo had started worshipping any gods, they seem to have kept quiet about it until taking the slow or sudden decision to build one gigantic temple.

As farmers, they would hope, or wish, for the seasons to continue with timely predictability – for the sun to shine hotly in summer, but less intensely in winter… for rain to maintain their supply of water, to feed the animals and to soften the earth and encourage plant growth… for relief from both heat and rain in what modern Gozitans call 'the shoulder months' when they could comfortably plant seeds or bring in harvests.

This could (very loosely) translate as a form of 'worship' or 'prayer' for the seasons and, with them, of course, fertility.

It is easy, from a distance of several thousand years, to assume that their pagan 'god', if prehistoric mankind had one, would be the sun, around which they might have believed that their lives, and perhaps the earth, revolved. Certainly Stonehenge, and Ġgantija itself, appear to be built as though to acknowledge the rising sun.

Even today in Għajnsielem, the most commonly heard prayer (outside a Catholic church building) is *Viva Xemx*, meaning 'long live the sun'...

But note that the building had no windows. If you are going to create the equivalent of a cathedral to honour the sun in all its glory, do you build it in a way that sunlight cannot get in to?

If they had used the stars to navigate their sea-crossing, they may also have had 'faith' in the stars. (They could have observed the planets, or some of them, through a hole in the uncompleted roof.)

One theory is that the different buildings are aligned with different celestial aspects of the night sky – a claim that could be made about the direction of all the front doors in any modern village chosen at random.

Or, perhaps, the nearest they came to what we would recognise as organised 'religion' was to celebrate birth and to venerate death. In that case, they had hopes and faith in fertility – both in their harvests and in animal and human reproduction (and perhaps of a life after death).

Their early statues are famously of (fat) women, but mainly of the breeding parts of their bodies – the breasts and hips. Their legs, heads and arms appear to be less relevant.

The ground plan – a circle above two other circles, all with domed roofs – has been interpreted as possibly replicating a woman's head and breasts. The fact that the entrances to Ġgantija and several (but not all) successive structures face south-east, can be seen as marking the 'birth' of the day, with the rising sun. When two extra circles were added there was no conflict with the human form theory: the new lobes would represent the thighs of the great maternal figure.

There is some evidence that the central 'aisles' of the temples which connect the 'breasts' to the entrance were painted with red ochre which might replicate the birth channel and go some way to supporting that fertility theory.

All this has been interpreted as the worship of 'Mother Earth'.

It may be so.

But it may be of some passing interest to note that before the so-called temples there were no 'Fat Lady' figures. If the temples were to be in her honour, it might be reasonable to assume that she would have appeared somewhere in effigy, first.

It may also be worth noting that the first 'modern' Gozitans who discovered the carvings assumed that they depicted the people responsible for the buildings – not that they were unknown deities who were worshipped inside them.

Although the female statues are the best known, they account for fewer than 20 per cent of the total number of figurines and statues that have been found. There are more depictions of phalluses than of breasts or vaginas. All this supports the theory of recognising and even actually 'praying' for continued fertility – animal, arable and of course human.

Breasts, vaginas and phalluses might be the visible representations of it. So 'Earth Mother', perhaps, rather than 'Mother Earth' which, in any case, is surely another more modern concept.

Do farmers 'worship' the earth? It seems unlikely.

There would be no need to build and attend a church to admire an 'Earth Mother' – every family had one, at home.

So desperate are the adherents to the idea of the giant structures being places built to worship and of 'rituals' that they do not even appear to have paused to consider one small element of human behaviour…

Potters were casting vessels and utensils in clay on a fairly regular – maybe, at times, even on an industrial – basis. At the end of each bout of production one might assume that there would be bits of clay left over. What would be more natural than that the children would have been allowed to play with it, while it was soft? And what would be the most likely shape that they would create, if not a human form?

Many of the statues (including those of some 'fat' ladies) are no more than a few inches tall, some as small as 7.5cm (3 inches), suggesting that the clay used was no more than the over-matter. Surely nobody was going to settle down to craft a statue – a 'figurine' – of their god in such tiny proportions and then fire up a kiln for it.

And then, following this seemingly hitherto unexplored likelihood, the clay could have been played with by potters of varying ages and levels of artistic skills, and only the more sophisticated examples would be preserved, while the dross, or most of it, probably found its way into the *torba*, lost for eternity.

And – no more than a passing thought – might not the young men watching the artisans have chipped a column of rock or rolled a handful of clay into a cylinder and cast it in the shape of a penis, as a form of 'laddish' behaviour?

If the settlers were looking for a deity, they could just as easily have worshipped 'the god of the sea', on whom their economy as farmers and traders necessarily depended. At a later time Bronze Age Greeks would have a name for him: *Poseidon*, who some civilisations believed was the husband of 'the earth mother'. He was also the creator of volcanic eruptions, while his wife (whose name has not been immortalised) controlled inland streams and springs.

They would require his beneficence for their vital cross-sea trading and communication.

At what stage does 'hope' become 'prayer'?

In fairness, and to support the supposition that Gozo's Neolithic community had somehow found religion, it could be noted that around the same time – say 3000BC – the distant Egyptians were creating an effectual pantheon of gods, with deities covering virtually every aspect of life.

The main Egyptian god was the sun-god, and they also built 'temples' to some of their divine manifestations, although access to them was restricted to the priesthood; people did their worshipping in their own homes.

However there is no evidence of any external influences on the Maltese islands and in any case ancient Egyptians were several stages behind Gozo on the religious and 'temple-building' timeline.

From what is known about maritime navigation of the era it is unlikely that the islanders could have known anything about what exotic deities might have been developing many miles across the sea in northern Africa, or elsewhere.

Realistically, there are two possible types of religion that could be said with any likelihood to have been prevalent on ancient Gozo: the one above ground that celebrated fertility (and reproduction and childbirth)…

And another, mostly below ground, venerating death.

However, once it had been decided that Ġgantija was a 'temple' the earliest examiners of the site knew what they were looking for.

A Temple...?

If Ġgantija was a temple ('a place of worship'), and any smaller single building was therefore a 'shrine', the three lobes of the basically clover-leaf floor plan would have to be 'apses' – which, handily, are usually semi-circular or D-shaped recesses of a church, with an altar from which the clergy can operate. In modern church architecture apses are separated from the rest of the church by a 'transept', and on this plan that would be the 'stalk' of the clovers.

[Incidentally, 'church' is a word and a concept that is purely Christian, while an 'apse', as a religious recess, is probably a (pre-Christian) Roman architectural invention.]

When Ġgantija was first extended (to a 'five-leafed clover' design) it involved more 'apses', but it was not felt necessary to connect the successive (north) chamber – another five apses – to the original building. In the extension, the innermost 'leaf' was too small to be recognised as an 'apse', so was dismissed by archaeologists as a mere 'niche'.

But David Trump, who appears to be a sort of godfather of

modern Maltese archaeology, declared confidently that 'these were surely temples'. And that appears to have been the end of any argument or reasoning among his acolytes.

So, at Ġgantija we are looking at a 'temple' that comprises only apses and altars, presumably to be occupied by 'priests' (or priestesses?), with little or no remaining space left for a congregation to… congregate. That might seem to have been a serious error in design.

Oh, but there was space outside. There was a terrace on which people could gather – and perhaps marvel and wonder about what might be going on inside the splendid building that they had created with their own, and their forefathers', toil and sweat… but into which they were probably not permitted. After all, there would be no room for them inside it.

(There was a stone bench around the wall on which they could sit, while they waited – perhaps to hear what some 'god' was declaring to their 'priests' at two dozen different 'altars'.)

And the population would congregate on the terrace… when? In the heat of summer? In the damp cold of winter? During harvest or sowing time? In daytime, or in darkness?

When would they desert their lands and trek from distant parts of even a small island, to 'worship' some person or some thing – effectively on a second-hand basis?

[At a much later time in history, generations of the

committed congregation of Roman Catholics in Għajnsielem, which was then part of the parish of Nadur, grew weary of the regular slog uphill to their church and built a statue within their growing village in front of which they could perform their regular devotions closer to home.]

Drawing of altars in an 'apse' at Ġgantija - 1848

In any case, it is surely unsafe to transfer our more modern traditions onto prehistoric communities. There is nothing anywhere to support the idea of a Neolithic need for this agricultural community to 'go to church', and certainly not of the necessity to so painstakingly build one.

There is no hard evidence in European man's early history of the existence of any actual 'gods'.

Perhaps the superstition of coincidences should not be overlooked – if we do this, the sun will shine… if we do this, the rain will fall… Maybe there was a celestial father (or mother) watching their every move.

Otherwise there would no common understanding among these farmworkers and weavers and potters of what a 'god' was, and what its function might be.

And if Neolithic man invented a 'god' for himself, he would not know that he needed to build and to attend a temple to make contact with it.

The early Christians, for example – who at least had a firm idea of why and to whom they were praying – did not build 'churches'; instead they met in each other's houses. There is no rational reason to believe that religiously minded Stone Age Gozitans (if any such people existed) would not, or could not, have done the same.

It would not be until mediaeval times (between the eleventh and fourteenth centuries after Christ's birth) that Christian parish churches and cathedrals began to be erected on a grand scale. Even then, these buildings would often be used as meeting places for the general community, for public banquets or the performance of early theatre, or for fairs and markets, and even as places to thresh and store grain.

[The oldest surviving place of Christian worship on Gozo, the small chapel dedicated to *'Santa Cecilie del Mugiarro'* – erected at the other side of the main road from the 'mud hut' settlement, and built around 1540 – has the marks of a threshing circle plainly visible on its floor. And *Tal-Qighan*, in the stone-built area of the same settlement, means 'threshing floor'.]

But the fact that Ġgantija was divided into small sections, and that the second, extending, 'temple' is not connected to the first, indisputably signifies that – whatever its prime purpose – it was not for 'communal' assembly. Rather, it appears to have been designed to create privacy for small groups, who might sometimes be attending, separately, at the same time.

And yet… the archaeologists who arrived on the scene with the preconception that these buildings were places of religious worship would even conclude that a number of pottery pieces found nearby, in what seemed to be a dump, were religious 'offertory bowls' that had been smashed 'to prevent their use in a secular context' by people who might find them.

Meanwhile, other pieces of pottery found elsewhere that had been used for dating this era of prehistory on Gozo were simply what they looked like… broken pieces of domestic pottery.

Just like the creation of a folk story, everything could be made to fit the plot.

*

Priests and Oracles

It might be worthwhile to pause momentarily and consider the concept of the early 'clergy' in the archaeological scenario.

For a temple we need a 'priest', a religious leader (and another word handily borrowed from Christianity that, at the time building started, would enter the vocabulary some 3,600 years in the future; a 'rabbi', a term in earlier use, had followed the line of Moses, who wasn't born yet, and it was always a part-time occupation).

Priests perform rituals and modern archaeologists refer to 'ritual' ceremonies being performed within the underground burial caves, and even to 'ritual' forms of animal sacrifices. Not surprisingly, there is not a jot of evidence of any such ritual practice, but the experts assume it and proclaim it, so it must be so.

Apparently after initial burial, skeletons were 'ritually' dismembered – to create more space for fresh bodies. They even coined a word for it: it had to be 'de-conception' – that is, the actual opposite of conception, the start of being.

Whatever it is called, it is a practice that continues today in family tombs in Malta.

The bones of earlier generations are moved and rearranged

in the bottom of a grave in order to make space for each new coffin. But that is not a priestly or religious ritual: it is a task that is performed by the cemetery's grave digger.

However, allowing for the suggestion that there would be a priest, why would he (or she), at Ġgantija, need three, then five, then ten separate 'altars'? A priest could operate from only one at a time. (And why were the 'altars' usually divided into three sections?)

Or do ten altars indicate the appointment and presence of ten 'priests'? All performing their temple-associated rituals at the same time …? Surely not.

Would the priesthood be an elected position? Would the first priest have been the first person – probably long forgotten before the buildings were even started – on the island who 'found god', the farmer (or farmer's wife) who 'got religion' and somehow managed to convert the others to it…? And then persuaded so many of them of the need to erect a magnificent temple?

Or would the role be an inherited profession?

Effective management of such a building, taking hundreds of years to build and to be constantly enlarged, would be a full-time job for a succession of people covering many generations.

Would that person have been the 'priest'?

*

Figure in a pleated skirt reconstructed from fragments found at Tarxien which some archaeologists suggest depicts a priest (or priestess). It would have stood about 30cm tall.

What Ġgantija needed, during its construction and for the arrangements of bodies and the rearrangement of already buried bones, was a site manager. Not a priest.

It was probably not a job suitable for anyone who would be otherwise useful as a farm worker.

There were circular holes in some of altar walls and these, for the temple-fixated, had to be 'oracle holes'.

Again, modern academics were thrusting later religious history (and ritual) onto the simple farming folk of Gozo.

An oracle hole, in classical antiquity, was a place at which divine advice or prophecy was sought. And the 'oracle' was a priest or priestess acting as a medium through whom advice or prophecy was sought from the gods. (*Oxford English*.)

In classical European history it had always been assumed that oracles were a creation of the ancient Greeks, most notably in Delphi, and around 500BC. If the analysts of Ġgantija are correct in their interpretations, it would appear that the Gozitan builders were about 3,000 years ahead of the game.

Would the 'oracle' be the same person as the 'priest' – prophesying through a hole in a wall, rather than from the altar or on the temple steps?

The reader can draw his own conclusions.

*

Animal Sacrifice?

Evidence of fires in some of the 'apses', and in one case the skeletal remains of a dog, and near it, a knife, 'suggest signs of animal sacrifice'.

It is not known why dogs were kept. Remains were insufficient in number to imply that they were being eaten. So perhaps they were 'sheepdogs' (dogs appear to have a natural tendency to round up other animals and, come to that, humans). They may have been guard dogs, but in either case as puppies they could easily have been family pets.

It seems somehow unlikely that a working farmer would give up his sheep-dog or guard-dog – and, even probably less so, a family pet – for 'sacrifice'.

How, to the uneducated mind, would 'animal sacrifice' work? If you slit the throat of a goat (or a dog) is that likely to bring on sunshine – or if you kill a pig will it bring rain?

These people had never read a book, had any form of religious education, never seen a movie or watched a television documentary.

Where does the idea of 'animal sacrifice' (another 'ritual') come from? Which farmer was voluntarily going to be prepared to sacrifice – literally – one of the animals on which his near-subsistence farming life depended?

In one 'temple', on Malta, a cavity was 'stuffed with the bones of domestic animals', and a long flint blade was found. The nearby stone block therefore obviously 'suggested a sacrificial altar'.

Or – this is no more than this writer's conjecture – maybe the people who revered human death held some of their animals in equally high regard. Perhaps they brought them into the 'temple' at the end of their lives as a sign of respect.

From wall carvings it is clear – as if there might be any doubt about it – just how important (or interesting) their animals were to the farmers.

There is, for example, an etched illustration of a bull, politely described as being 'very male', and another of a sow with 14 piglets at suck.

These are both obvious signs of a recognition of 'fertility', although not necessarily a mark of devotion to our 'Mother Earth'.

No farmer would give up a breeding animal because somebody with an implausible idea of a new religion told him that killing the productive beast would change the weather, or would guarantee a better harvest next year.

Whereas to sacrifice an impotent bull or a barren sow would surely be disrespectful to the unknown 'god'.

*

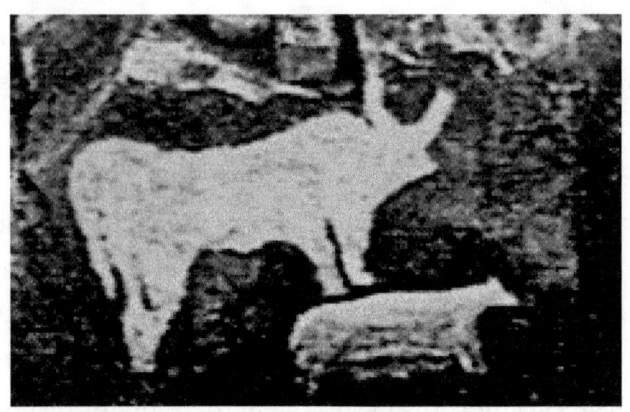

Bull and Sow etching (Tarxien)

Although animal sacrifices can be made to fit the theory, like so much else about the temples and the temple builders' lives that relies on supposition and on sheer guesswork, or on the most likely interpretation, it ain't necessarily so.

The cinders could have been signs that in winter the buildings needed heating. Perhaps sometime in the 5,000 years between a building's abandonment and its discovery a dog had wandered inside it and died there. Perhaps a careless workman had dropped his sharpened piece of flint, as so many kitchen workers appear to have discarded their cooking pots and utensils.

There were, let's not forget, plenty of human skeletons that were also in the proximity of the pre-historic fireplaces or hearths. But that fact has not 'suggested' to our modern, civilised, researchers that cannibalism or human sacrifices were practised.

Yet to an interpreter of artefacts who is obsessed by the idea of ritual, every possibility – human or animal – can be made to fit the picture, however unlikely it might appear to a more rational, or cynical, or doubting mind.

*

...Or a Mausoleum?

The theory that Ġgantija building was intended to be funeral-related is supported by the choice of the site, directly in line – each about 400 yards apart – with the Circle and Santa Verna.

In fact, archaeologists are moving away from calling it 'the Xagħra Circle' because they suspect there may be other 'circles', as yet undiscovered, within the area. It is now being called the Xagħra Hypogeum. Other sites, notably two caves (the 'North Cave'' and Ta' Ghejzu) within a few metres of Ġgantija, have been excavated and produced more human and animal skeletons.

Perhaps, if the perfectly reasonable suggestion that the early Gozitan communities actually honoured their dead were recognised as being their most important – and maybe even only – form of 'religion', Ġgantija would have been erected as a *mausoleum* ('a stately or impressive building housing a tomb or group of tombs.' – *Oxford English*.)

It is this writer's contention that each so-called 'temple' was more likely to have been what would nowadays be described as a 'chapel of rest' for the dead.

The bodies could have been laid out on what have otherwise been described as altars in the D-shaped side chapels, with sufficient space for viewing, and for preparing for burial, and for friends and family members to gather and pay their respects. This is sometimes nowadays called a 'visitation', and is an interim stage before final burial elsewhere. It would have been, or could have been, a place for important funerary ritual – if any form of 'ritual', beyond veneration or respect were required.

And the holes in the walls… (this is only a passing thought) could have been viewing holes for family members too timid to approach their deceased relatives closely or directly.

As the bodies started to wither or the space was needed for fresher corpses – as the population (and with it, the number of deaths) increased – the eventual burial would have taken place a short distance away.

Again, what doesn't fit, or make logical sense, about that? Perhaps even more logical sense than that the building was a place of worship (that is, unless it were for honouring, or even 'worshipping' the dead).

Decomposing with time, their spirits by now being considered to be well on their way to their afterlife, the skeletons were shoved further back into the caves to make space for newer corpses to be added. As already noted, it happens today.

And their funerary ornaments, no longer required for their final journey, were stacked with them, or close to them.

The burial places came first, the temples came next.

The 'fat ladies', identified by some as tributes to a 'Mother Earth' came last.

So… Ġgantija Mausoleum… Malta's Mausoleum Period… The Mausoleum Builders…?

Maybe the history books and the guide books need to be rewritten. Except that it just doesn't sound so grand. Nor even quite so appealing and inviting to tourists.

Temple or mausoleum? Whichever is the case, there is as yet no hard evidence to support argument either for it or against it.

A case could probably equally be made for Ġgantija being built as Gozo's first general hospital: after all, there was no known form of surgery, but the injured or dying could have been taken there – and there were burial grounds nearby.

The skeletons don't show any obvious signs of the sort of diseases that affect bones. There were a few broken toes – hardly surprising with the amount of rock moving taking place – and some identifiable cases of arthritis, but generally the people were in a relatively healthy physical state, suggesting that their diet was satisfactory. So quite possibly they were just worn out with all the hard physical work.

Not so much an infirmary, then, as a place for the dying, or nearly dead. A final place to rest before the absolutely final resting place in a communal cave.

Yet another theory for which the pieces could fit…

The Clover-leaf

Dating techniques have helped to establish when they were building: the Maltese Neolithic period covered roughly 3,000 years, from about 5600 to 2500BC. (It was followed by the Bronze Age.)

Of the surviving monuments, Ġgantija was built, or at least construction started on it, first. And successive buildings would generally copy the trefoil pattern – the symmetrical arrangement of D-shaped alcoves along a single axis.

There would be an impressive *trilithon* [three stones] – two giant stones supporting a third as a lintel to create the entrance – in the centre of the front elevation that often faced south-east and was intentionally curved. It may have been the first stage of building, along with the central aisle, perhaps built to face the rising sun, or to let in the most light… or maybe, and perhaps realistically, to protect the people standing outside it from the prevailing north-westerly wind.

The façade was then constructed of large upright stones called *orthostats* [orthos = straight; stat = standing] with the tallest ones at the extremities. Relatively smaller – although still massive – stone blocks were laid in horizontal courses on top of them.

Outside, a forecourt was usually levelled and filled with *torba*.

There was often a stone bench running along the base of the front wall.

Access to the interior was restricted. The semi-circular alcoves could accommodate no more than a small group of individuals.

One popular interpretation is that the community would sit or stand outside while 'secret rites' were performed inside by a religious elite of 'priests' (or of 'priestesses') on their behalf.

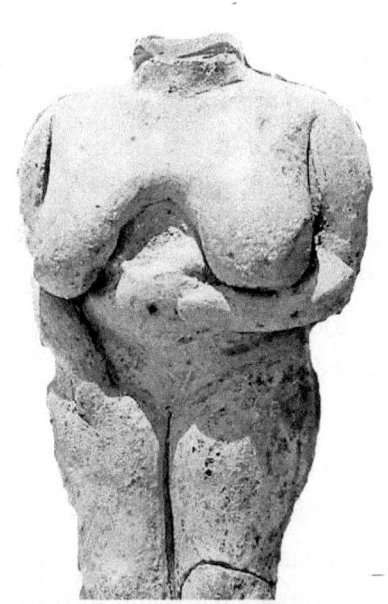

The 'Venus of Malta', from Hagar Qim (13cm tall)

Soft limestone carved into life-sized human phalluses is proof to some people that 'initiation ceremonies' were 'probably' conducted within the private sanctuary of the trefoil leaves or 'apses'.

Statues of women were seen as likely tributes to a goddess, perhaps to 'Mother Earth' (no doubt future archaeologists will interpret the Venus de Milo in a similar light!)

*

However, the reason why it was built, and the function for which it was intended, have become less important than the simple fact that Ġgantija *was* built. Perhaps it is better that its actual intended use remains an enigma.

Whatever the reason, or the excuse or the necessity, agreement was reached. The decision had been made to build it, on a windswept promontory that would later become known as Xagħra, Gozo.

There may have been a long gap between the choice of the burial sites and the decision to build a magnificent place for final viewing and funeral rites. Or it might mean that the argument or simple discussion, about whether such communal enterprise of any sort was needed, had persisted over 500 years or more before agreement was finally reached.

Perhaps, finally, the great architect or master builder – and there is no doubt that he was great because his creations were original and magnificent and observers several thousand years later would gaze at them in awe – said: 'Okay, friends, if we are going to do it, this is what it should look like,' while taking a stick and drawing a simple clover-leaf pattern in the soil at his feet.

He would have mapped out the first monumental free-standing stone building in the history of the world.

*

Construction

The site would have been marked out and the already accepted ground plan cut into the earth based on the agreed drawing. They would doubtless have stood back and admired even this very first phase in the construction of their dream building. Even at this preliminary stage, to the untrained masons who had previously built no more than low clusters of single and extended cottages and houses, the clover-leaf vision already in their minds' eyes must have appeared magnificent... gigantic.

Stage two would be the foundations. For this they would need the hard grey Upper Coralline rock.

This was no problem. They were going to build directly on to it.

But rocks of the Globigerina type needed for the more general building, and in need of most shaping and dressing, were in seriously short supply.

In fact, they were totally absent.

The big rocks would have to be sourced from outcrops in the valley below the plateau, well over a kilometre to the west... and then somehow dragged or manoeuvred up a steep slope to the building site.

Although legend would have us believe that the rocks were

moved to Xagħra from ta' Ċenċ, that supposition would have involved a journey of more than three kilometres.

We know that the early builders at *L-Imrejżbiet* (Għajnsielem) which was considerably closer, had been able to source both their hard and soft rock locally.

There was no shortage of Globigerina almost anywhere on the islands of Malta and Gozo – except within the immediate vicinity of the chosen plateau.

Already, at this first stage, there must have been some murmuring among members of the community who harboured, and probably expressed, doubts about the construction. Perhaps they had doubted the need for the project from the start.

All right, it had been agreed that they would build this impressive place. But would it not be a better idea to erect it in an area where they could more easily find the necessary rocks with which to build it?

Or even to abandon the plan entirely…?

Did the walls really need to be twice or three times the height of anything that had been built before it?

If there was a debate about whether to cancel or re-site it, or redesign it, the proposers obviously lost the argument. The decision was taken to press on, regardless.

But even the most experienced members of the team were merely builders in stone… not shifters of rock.

For their houses, for their floors and their giant cornerstones, and with help from their neighbours, they could roll even the heaviest rocks for a few yards, maybe even by working wooden levers and perhaps sledges underneath them.

This, or some relatively similar simple method, had sufficed at *L-Imrejżbiet*.

But to move heavy rocks for more than a mile, and also uphill …?

They couldn't know that in about 500 years their counterparts 1,300 miles away in England were going to build something in Wiltshire that would be called Stonehenge. And that the three-ton stones used for it would reputedly come from Pembroke, about 160 miles distant in Wales. Nor could they know that 5,000 years later schoolchildren would be taught that the problem was solved by rolling the massive stones on tree trunks, picking up the trunks as the stones were rolled over them and placing them at the front… up hills, across the summits, down hills, over plains and then floating them on rafts up the Bristol Channel. (A competing theory, not taught in schools, is that the stones were simply shifted to Wiltshire by a giant Ice Age glacier, some 20,000 years earlier, and they were already available locally when Neolithic man began building Stonehenge.)

Rolling on tree trunks – would that ever occur as a solution to people who had never had a primary school history lesson?

Prehistoric man is automatically seen as primitive. Not so on Gozo (and later on Malta). He may have been restricted to using hand-axes of local chert (the hardest of the coral stone) or imported flint, to knives and scrapers of obsidian, wedges of wood or stone, to stone pick-axes and hammers and wooden levers… but his use of them exhibited an amazing degree of sophistication that remains unexplained and awe-inspiring.

*

Invention

The near-total deforestation of Gozo had not yet been completed: that would come with the Bronze Age, and its need for wood fires and charcoal for metal-working. In 3600BC there should have been plenty of trees – the indigenous oak, ash and pine – still around. The trunks would need to be of a fairly regular size to make rolling big stones on them a practicality, but it could be done.

Construction was, after all, going to be a long-term project…

There was nobody on hand to teach them any of the techniques for moving and building with stone because nobody else had yet been faced with the problem.

The tree-trunk idea, if ever mooted, would be completely innovative in pre-historic times, and truly inspirational.

Thousands of years later it would be recognised as 'the invention of the wheel'… a development in the history of mankind on a level of importance with the understanding of the controlled use of fire.

We know that early man on Gozo was indeed inventive and intelligent.

Having first learnt the complexities of modern farming, he had learnt to sail and to navigate.

In the 2,000 or so years since his arrival he had taught himself how to clear a space for housing by excavating to rock level, learnt to mark out a floor plan, of the need to lay solid foundations, to make bricks out of clay and build walls with them, to invent a form of 'concrete', to prop up roofs, and then to build stone houses and make them weatherproof and even damp-proof.

In their isolated habitation they saw challenges, and they solved them. In short, they possessed creative genius.

So how would they move massive rocks?

Somebody – and this would be a person who deserves recognition in the history of the world – had one solution…

It was to chisel the hardest stones into spheres like big cannon balls. Beneath one of the heavy boulders they would of course simply be crushed or would sink into the earth, but, in sufficient numbers and, if placed on a plank of tree trunk to spread the weight, like a railway, it would be possible… And the local oaks could grow to 20m in height.

They had invented the 'ball-bearing': literally, balls of stone that would bear the weight of a giant rock.

This is not to say that Gozo's inspirational inventors were the first in the world to do anything (anything, that is, except creating 'the first free-standing stone building on earth'); different peoples in different parts of the world may have been having – or already have had – similar inspirational brainwaves. But it is worth repeating that 'the temple builders' were creating everything for the first time, because nobody they knew had the experience to tell them how to solve any of these problems.

And then they discovered that they could carve a thick disc of stone that could be inserted into a similarly-sized circular groove in a large boulder and then rotated, or 'wheeled'.

They had invented 'the wheel': made of stone, not of wood.

(So far as is known, they did not invent the 'wheelbarrow', which would have been useful, because they did not know about an axle. But if they could lift one end of a rock and wheel or roll the other end, they were not far away from that invention.)

Archaeologists have found the stone balls, the stone wheels and the carved sockets (well-worn and often eroded) that confirm that – whatever else might have been happening elsewhere in the world, and so whatever might be claimed by later historians for other prehistoric communities in other places – 'the wheel' and 'the ball-bearing' were both totally original inventions on Gozo.

It was going to be a long, hard slog. They must have realised that much. But they had worked out how to do it and the construction of Ġgantija eventually got under way.

Ġgantija!

Yet another thing that 'nobody knows' is when the building got its name.

The modern Maltese word for gigantic is *ġġanti*. But, the Maltese for a giant, like Sansuna, is *ġġant*. We do not know which version – the folk tale or archaeologically inspired 'history' – came first.

Gigantic, though, certainly describes the place, and it was also built of gigantic stones, often one giant rock on top of another giant rock. Nobody has yet worked out for sure how the builders managed to do that. Ropes and pulleys? Massive levers? Sheer unassisted man-power? Towing on wooden sledges by oxen? It becomes tiresome to repeat it, but nobody knows.

If some sort of early scientific solution or engineering device was applied, it has not been discovered.

Laying the foundations – cutting out the ground and digging out the soil down to a firm rock base, perhaps using shovels carved from oak – would have been relatively easy: the builders from Għajnsielem knew about doing that.

Moving stones for the first 'course' would be a difficult and strenuous task, although by using ball bearings and primitive 'wheels' and sledges it could gradually be achieved.

The stones of the outer walls had to be positioned precisely in line, alternately longitudinally and latitudinally, 'face'-out and edge-out, to ensure strength and stability. Somebody had worked out the logistics required for safely stacking giant rocks, one on top of the other, without the benefit of any form of bedding mortar. So there needed to be some form of mutual interlocking of the rough surfaces of the megaliths. And then they would be chipped with flint, inside and outside, to create smooth surfaces where they were visible.

Then came the second course, with yet more great stones, some of them the same size as the base, dragged to the site. They had solved the problem of getting them there, but how would they get them up on top of the first stones, some of them already standing upwards of 2m (6ft) tall?

There are archaeologists who are experts in Neolithic pottery, some are interested in the history of mankind and use the pottery as partial evidence. Some may be preoccupied by Stone Age religion and ancient gods.

Others are interested in the logic of pre-historic engineering. And this latter group, trying to put themselves into the mind-set of ancient Man while at the same time applying engineering 'logic', came up with a couple of possible solutions.

With a sufficient body of men and a sufficient number of sturdy wooden poles, each megalith could have been raised a few inches at a time and smaller rocks, and then increasingly bigger boulders, shoved underneath until the stone being raised was at the right height.

This would appear to be a painfully slow process, and also a dangerous practice, but it has been successfully tried by historical enthusiasts and proved to be a possibility.

A more likely – and more practical – solution is thought to be that the builders would have created ramps of hard stone and chippings and then shoved, pulled and towed the big rocks up the slope to the top, perhaps even using rolling logs, or balls or wheels of stone, to the top of the tall base megaliths onto which they could be slid to create the second layer.

Man-made ramps of rock… it is obvious, is it not? And the longer the ramp, the more gradual the slope up which they would have to tow, slide and to push upwards. They would need to move or to recreate the ramp after every endeavour, in order to place successive second-course stones. Or, perhaps to have only one ramp, and slide the second layer along the top of the first.

Again, it is important to remember that there was nobody around to teach this sort of engineering. It had never been attempted anywhere else.

Ggantija would be unique in its construction, and there was a mastermind on its building site who was solving problems as they cropped up.

Once again, the stones would need to be levered precisely into alignment to create a true vertical face, inside and outside the building. If they don't appear to be quite so flush today, that is the result of 5,000 years of erosion, not of casual building techniques.

Another factor that they needed to take into account was that, with so massive a footprint, the walls needed to slope inwards as they went higher, resulting in the creation of a smaller area for them to be able to create a roof.

This they did, by 'corbelling' the upper walls – that is, building a series of inverted steps to reduce the space, and start enclosing the roof.

Then there are three theories about the roof: that it was closed with a 'capping stone' (that would have needed to be about 5m across, and has never been found, on any site); that it was finished with wood and clay that would have deteriorated over the centuries; or that it was left open to let in light – the building, remember, had no windows. But it had drainage.

And then, who told them about corbelling? Certainly, nobody in Sicily was erecting buildings with corbelled roofs. They must have invented the technique, solved the problem of the tensile strength of the indigenous stones, themselves.

Again, the master builder must have experimented with, or found some way of calculating, the strength before deciding on corbelling.

Another feat of original architectural engineering.

And then the central aisle needed to slope towards the entrance – for drainage, because the roofs were not going to be watertight.

The entrance to the north chamber: paved with slabs and sloped to allow for drainage

The fact that there were no windows and was therefore no interior light source, that the central aisle was sloped for drainage from the start, and that there were hearths beneath the centre of the open roofs, suggests (to this writer) that the corbelled roofs were never intended to be 'capped'.

All this work would have required a project manager – quite likely more than one. Somebody needed to assign jobs to the farmers who turned up each working day to join the building force, and to oversee every part of each job's completion.

It might be assumed that strong women would work alongside the men – why not? After all, they were going to be credited in folk-history as having been the sole builders – while the less muscular of both sexes stayed home and got on with the always necessary tasks of milking cows, sheep and goats, cooking, weaving, sowing crops, scraping hides, making pottery, planting and picking vegetables…

On site the managers needed people who could identify the Globigerina stone that would be suitable for their needs, and others (maybe the same team) to excavate it… more to load it onto whatever form of balls, rollers or sledges they were using… a large number of strong bodies or oxen to pull, or of people to push, it uphill to the part of the site where it was needed… a team creating the ramps, and gradually moving them along the walls…

Inside the building, a crew laying a *torba* floor… and another set of stone-masons working on internal walls and the 'altars' or tables.

Eventually, a workforce would be required to remove all trace of the ramps' existence… a team of decorators and plasterers would infill the inner walls with clay, plaster them with a smooth mixture similar to fine *torba* flooring, and then paint them…

And hopefully some form of workers' canteen to provide refreshment and sustenance (and perhaps also to attend to any number of inevitable cuts and bruises).

It is important, in considering the ingenuity of the 'temple-builders' to keep in mind that these people were farmers, first, and not construction workers or engineers.

And yet among their tiny community they found people who could design a magnificent edifice, could organise a massive work-force, could work as planners and problem solvers… and then there were movers, lifters and straighteners and decorators of giant rocks who quite clearly had the ability to work as teams.

Which brings us back to the always vital fact that their prime job was food production. In fact, to maintain their economy the farmers needed to over-produce their output in order to be able to exchange it for the necessary equipment, such as flint and obsidian (and paint) for producing what would one day become their masterpiece…

The definitive showcase of prehistoric Stone Age humanity.

So, farming – ploughing and the production of crops and the husbandry and eventual food and skin elements of animals – which is usually considered to be a full-time job, had always to remain as the priority.

At the start of the (modern calendar) year they would be making and mending tools, repairing walls, digging and clearing ditches, ploughing and then carrying and spreading manure over the fields and planting spring vegetables. In spring there would be the first crops and then the ploughing of fallow fields, harrowing [breaking up clods of earth], sowing and scattering seeds for crops, and probably shearing sheep for wool.

In early summer they would be weeding the arable fields and hay-making.

During predictable spells of fine weather at least some of them would need to sail to Sicily with their surplus production and their hides and probably their unique styles of pottery and weaving, and sail back with vital pieces of farming – and now of building – equipment. In the middle of the year there would probably be no grass at all, nor very much visible that was still green, and the livestock would need to survive on stored hay, and maybe also on saved water.

As soon as the new cereals were ready there would be crop-cutting and gathering of the harvest, threshing of corn and more ploughing of fields, most likely followed by the annual slaughter of animals for food, some of which had to be smoked or otherwise preserved, perhaps using salt, plus preparation of skins and hides for leather.

Throughout the year there would be random but routine veterinary events such as lambing, calving and foaling, the care and treatment of sick livestock as well as a constant preparedness for unexpected changes in the weather.

And every day there would be milking. Farming is a 24/7 occupation.

So when did they find time for building?

*

The archaeological engineers on the case first made a few assumptions, and then made calculations based on them.

In a dissertation that earned him a PhD from Bristol University, Daniel Clark, who had a background in engineering, reckoned that to put the biggest stones into position would require the strength of maybe 50 men. He estimated that to erect only the main building, the 'south temple', would take more than 15,500 man/days (which presumably means that 155 men, working non-stop, could have built it in 100 days... little more than three months).

That does not seem unreasonable, except that it would require maximum degrees of both efficiency and organisation, and all working at the same time (which would be impractical); and in any case Stone Age agricultural life was not that simple.

The total available labour force could never have been kept on the job for any successive number of full days because of its essential occupation with food production. The numbers of stone-movers and lifters and positioners who were both willing and able to leave their fields – perhaps bringing their oxen with them – must have fluctuated widely on a day-to-day basis.

Certainly, the strenuous work would not be carried out during the intense heat of high summer, nor in the fixed seasons for sowing and harvesting or, say, lambing. And because of the unpredictability of agricultural life, no volunteer could guarantee, with absolute assurance, that he would be available for construction work on any given day. It must have been frustrating for whoever had been put in overall charge of the project to be unsure about the size of the team able to work for him on a daily routine.

How many people might have been available for the building work?

Estimates of prehistoric population figures are always going to be uncertain, but let us assume around 1,000 people lived on Gozo during the building period. That might mean an average of 100 people, ten nuclear families, living in each of ten settlements (there are currently 15 parishes on the island). Although whether any single farmstead community could have supported 100 people is a matter of complete guesswork and so it might appear to be on the generous side.

Let us assume that on one random day 200 of them reported for work at the site.

Some would be required for ramp-building and regular maintenance, using bamboo baskets to carry rocks and earth and dump and pack it firmly in the required position.

Others would be filling and laying and tamping the *torba*.

The strongest 50 of them would be tasked with the excavation and then the movement of a single big rock. They could move it a few yards uphill in a single day. But only a few yards at a time; the positioning and placing would be many days later.

Obviously, if 100 strong citizens turned up, they could move two rocks a short distance ... (100 men could not move a single rock twice as far as 50, because they would get under each other's feet).

However, the notion that 20 per cent of the estimated total (male and female) population would be able and willing, first, to make the journey to Xagħra and then to volunteer to employ all their strength on a project with little to show for it at the end of the day seems unlikely (at least, to this writer).

Of course, a farmer who is totally organised with helpers can allow himself a day off from working the land or attending his herds. But would he rather spend it on a well-earned rest, putting his feet up... or on shifting rocks?

And then there is the question of our 'random day'. If only 25 strong men turn up for work, they are going to make little or no impression on the movement of any of the big stones.

If one assumes that the only time available and suitable for construction work would be during the three-month winter period, it would require a sufficient number to turn up on the same day – ideally on a day when it was not raining.

And if they had abandoned the work and returned to it the following winter it might well appear that their previous effort had contributed little. It would be even more discouraging if the stones they moved had slid back downhill in their absence.

They surely knew that they were creating a masterpiece that would endure for many centuries. At some stage they must have realised that they would not live to see its completion.

Maintaining enthusiasm for the project and for its seemingly endless construction may have been the biggest job of all.

There were to be many more complications – not least the fact that, as the three-leaf clover plan of the first temple appeared to be nearing completion, the decision would be taken that it was too small to serve its original purpose – whatever it was – and needed to be extended to almost double its original size.

When the now-extended job was finished, any rough fronts and edges of the façades chipped off and the inside floors laid and the walls smoothly 'plastered' and painted, the entire community could turn up on a day out with their families and admire their magnificent – gigantic – work.

Perhaps only then would they be told that it was too small and two more leaves had to be added, so that the first part of the building, which would become known as 'the south temple', would then have five 'apses'.

They would have to start again.

For what possible reason? For the unexpected appointment of two more 'priests'?

Or to deal with an increasing number of deaths?

Later still, part of the massive (7m high) wall surrounding it had to be dismantled so that an additional, but unconnected, building (yet another original trefoil plan) that would itself require extension before satisfactory completion, and would later be called the 'north temple', could be erected beside it.

There is evidence of work commencing on a third building, although only the façade appears to have been started on, before that construction was finally abandoned.

By carbon-dating of different parts of it, archaeologists agree that completion of the entire project, the double-temple edifice whose remains would be visible and commanding awe maybe 5,000 years later, would have taken 600 to 1,000 years. Or even longer – because the fact is that it would never be finished.

It is perfectly reasonable to wonder whether the succeeding generations had all shared the degree of enthusiasm that the original taskforce of their ancestors must have held.

Even though it could be assumed that they were now being born into a tradition in which agriculture necessarily came first, but construction work was always to be a close second occupation, with family members toiling side by side on the site, human nature must have caused many, down the centuries, to question its absolute necessity, as originally envisaged by their forefathers. Or perhaps religious fervour (if that was the driving force) increased as successive generations evolved, creating an inherent determination to finish the job, however difficult and time-consuming it was.

Below, three altars in one of the 'apses' and an aerial view of the 'site, showing the (top down) design of the extended 'clover-leaf' pattern

Melita

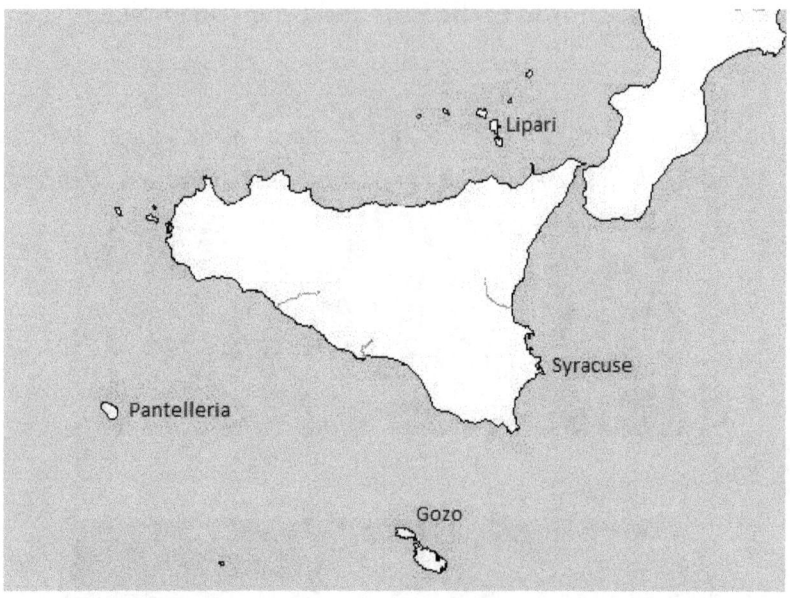

While, or very shortly after, the Sicani/Sicilians had started to occupy Gozo, more of their tribe had arrived on the island of Malta, and had settled there.

The Romans, when they invaded many years later, would name it Melita, in reference to the Greek word for honey – perhaps because of the island's unique native species of bee. (And part of the daily diet of the giantess Sansuna.)

With only *il-Fliegu* [the Channel] to separate them, there would obviously be regular trade and communication between the two islands.

There is clear evidence that while Gozitans were sourcing their black obsidian volcanic glass from Lipari (although not necessarily directly from that island, since it was traded elsewhere on Sicily), some of their southern neighbours had acquired the greener version of it from Pantelleria – another small and uninhabited island south of Sicily, although not in a direct line with the Maltese islands and about 200km (125 miles) distant from them.

It is doubtful whether the settling Maltese could have known about, and found, Pantelleria other than by accident. It is a similar distance (62m, 100km) from Sicily, so could probably be visible from a hilltop on a clear day from there, and would have appeared as interesting and as worthy of exploration as Gozo had been. But although the soil there was fertile, it was intensely volcanic and had no sources of fresh water so was not, so to speak, deemed fit for human habitation.

Another (unlikely) possibility is that a ship, blown off its original course for Gozo by unexpected cross-winds, simply stumbled across Pantelleria. In which case there would be a possibility that the crew filled their craft with as much obsidian as they could safely carry, and sailed back to Sicily to trade it, then perhaps restarted their voyage.

Or even that, having discovered such a rich source of the tradeable product, they abandoned their ideas of discovery and created a new business of importing it.

Obsidian glass was a vital tool for prehistoric man who needed something hard enough and sufficiently sharp for cutting and scraping. It was found in Pantelleria and in Lipari (and in Sardinia well out of reach of, and probably unknown by, the Maltese settlers).

The three sources of obsidian were sufficiently different that their place of origin could be determined by looking at glass samples (and later being confirmed by chemical analysis).

With little navigational ability – the compass was yet to be invented – it would seem unlikely that they would be able to sail from Malta and find Pantelleria to restock. In any case, at around only 60 miles away, Sicily was much closer – and by heading in any northward direction from Gozo, impossible to miss.

So the likelihood seems to be that both Pantellarian and Liparian obsidian would have been sourced from Sicily.

Some time after building of Ġgantija had started, the neighbours in the south started to build their own 'temple' clusters (some of which would be described by archaeologists as having been 'converted later into housing' although some of them appear to have been houses before the 'temples' were built….

Most of them copied the trefoil pattern (with an external terrace) as their ground plan, and followed similar styles of design and construction.

It was to be the start of an obsession with 'temple building'. Construction was gradually becoming more sophisticated, as exemplified by the immense stone blocks and intricate facades of the buildings, each one intentionally better and more ornate than the last – much as would happen with local Maltese and Gozitan Christian parish church buildings several millennia later – each village wanting a bigger and better church than the last one.

The Maltese – and the term is used here to differentiate that island's settlers from the Gozitans – built generally high walls with similarly ingeniously structured corbelled roofs that would not be totally completed and with the final, centre, part of the roofing believed by some to have been covered with animal skin. (At least, no capping stones have been found and wood, skin and clay coverings would not have survived the rigours of centuries).

Again, it is also perfectly possible that, although narrowed against the rain and the burning sunshine, the roofs could have been left open for light, or for a natural extraction of smoke from the hearths.

The earliest of Malta's Neolithic building sites could have been the Ħal Saflieni hypogeum in 3300-3000BC, by which time construction of Ġgantija was well under way, and the

Xagħra burial sites well established, and there is absolutely no doubt about its purpose.

Three storeys deep with underground caves as burial chambers, it has intriguing red ochre paintings and carvings on its walls. Several thousand skeletons were found inside it, along with some of their personal items and pottery. The only prehistoric underground 'temple' in the world, it is accessed via Burial Street, in Paola.

The peak of the Maltese 'temple-building' phase was around 3000-2500BC. There was a lot of it on the south island, including Ħaġar Qim, Mnajdra, Borg in-Nadur, Bugibba, Tas-Silġ and Tarxien, while evidence of domesticity was sometimes more apparent on Gozo (the confusion continuing to be the description of any stone building as a 'temple'.

Ħaġar Qim

The Maltese word *ħaġar*, meaning stones, can also imply a site surrounded by stone walling (it was the original name for the walled settlement at the foot of the *castrum* – the Citadel hill in Victoria, Gozo). The root word then appears in the names of the sites Ħaġar Qim and Ta' Ħaġrat. The word *Qim* in Maltese implies veneration.

Tirix, from which the place-name Tarxien derives, also means stone, or large stone [a 'megalith']. *Mnajdra* in Arabic means a plot of ground with planted trees.

Most of the names used to refer to the different sites are expressive but none is as impressive as Ġgantija.

*

Archaeology

This dissertation ends logically with the completion (or abandonment) of so-called 'temple building' on Gozo, and also on Malta.

But it would be unreasonable to leave unanswered the obvious question: 'So... What happened next?' And also: 'What happens next?'

The dating and understanding of the various phases of activity in the temples has not been easy. The main problem found was that the sites themselves are evolutionary in nature, in that each successive temple brought with it alteration and sometimes further refinement to architectural development.

Furthermore, in some cases, later Bronze Age peoples built their own sites over the Neolithic temples, thus adding an element of confusion to early researchers who did not have modern dating technology.

And then along came the archaeologists...

Even the best and keenest of them, maybe the most learned professionals of their day, were unintentionally responsible for destroying evidence that would have been useful to the modern generation with scientific dating and methods of sifting and interpreting the smallest remnants of matter.

Sites were rifled – often with the best intentions – without proper dating and recording. And in the meantime (and the sites were abandoned for upwards of 3,000 years) people came, looked, and took away some pieces that appeared interesting and might even be valuable.

It is generally accepted that the 'discovery' of the chain of megalithic structures occurred in the 1800s (AD), although some had been noted by travellers as far back as the 17th century. And they would of course have been known to all the islanders, who were perhaps no more than bemused by them.

The 19th and early 20th centuries saw the first actual 'archaeological' examinations, although in modern terms these were less than scientific. There were even some attempts at reconstruction, with heavy stones that appeared to have fallen being lifted back into what was presumed to have been their original place.

And earth mounds were removed from the sites that could have contained evidence that might later have been useful to the modern professionals with their sieving and dating equipment.

It is important to understand that even today there is no such thing as an archaeological 'flying squad'.

When artefacts – say a stash of pottery – are reported to the responsible authority by a citizen with a sense of duty (who, although it seems unlikely, might be a farmer, uncovering them while ploughing his field), it takes a long time before anything happens. A very long time.

A find of potentially prehistoric material does not get immediately encompassed in a tent and the area around it cordoned off.

It is not at all like a crime scene on the TV.

In the meantime, friends of the finder go to look at the site and will pick up 'souvenirs'. They may keep them for display at home or take them to an auction house where the 'experts' will, in all likelihood, identify pre-historic pottery as 'Phoenician'.

The visitors, having already collected the complete or least broken crockery that can be valued or sold, the archaeologists, when they turn up, will find only the broken pieces – the ubiquitous 'shards'…

(Caruana had complained that an 'interesting' tomb in Għajnsielem had 'already been rifled… and cleared of the greater part of its contents.')

When a potentially pre-historic site is discovered and reported, assuming that the professionals bother to examine the evidence, and the site, we might expect a report of the findings in a year, or maybe two or three years' time.

Things nowadays are far better than they were, even in very recent history. In 1964, to coincide with independence from British colonialism, the Maltese government closed the

Faculty of Arts at the University. A change of government in 1987 reopened it. In the intervening 23 years lecturers at the school of archaeology had been hanging around, with no students to teach.

The clay-brick structure found beside Mgarr-road in Gozo by Joe Attard Tabone in December 1984 was therefore not excavated until June 1987… and a 'preliminary' report was made in 1988.

After all, we had waited for up to 7,000 years for this. What difference does an additional year, or three, make, to a mud hut?

There is no running along the corridors of Academe.

*

The End of History

Between about 2400 and 2200 BC (which, at least in archaeological terms, means 'suddenly') everything stopped.

There is no specific evidence of life continuing on Gozo, nor even on Malta. No pottery, no building, no farming, no trading. Construction work on Ġgantija halted (after about 1,200 years' work) before the site had been finished.

'Temple building', which started at Ġgantija around 3600BC, seems to have fizzled out after Tarxien (on Malta) some time around 2500BC. And, apparently, so did 'civilisation' on the islands. At least, there is no sign of its having continued.

Where did it disappear to… and why?

Historians, guided by what the archaeologists tell them, have naturally come up with a number of possible explanations for such circumstances.

Probably the most far-fetched is that the 'priestly cult' declared the islands to have become 'ungodly' and ordered everybody to leave. This sounds fairly preposterous, except to those who are convinced that there ever was such a 'cult' on Gozo (and Malta). It fits with the idea of 'temples' with 'priests', of course, but there is no evidence anywhere of such a caste of people. And would they want to abandon their magnificent creation?

Alternatively, following much the same pattern, is the notion that the farmers became disillusioned or disaffected by the power of the 'priests', and quit the islands to escape from them.

While neither of these theories can be dismissed out of hand, it might be difficult to imagine families who had farmed a property for generations opting to leave it, either because they were ordered to or because they disagreed with some person or band of people with some sort of assumed authority.

There is no evidence of a power-structure on either island. While the architects and masons must have exercised some form of authority on occasions, and the potters were doubtless respected as craftsmen (or women), there is nothing to suggest a formal hierarchy of any kind. There are no visible signs of exceptional wealth, power or prestige.

Another possibility for the collapse of the 'temple society' is disease: an actual plague, wiping out the entire population (although in history most plagues rarely affected everybody, in any group of people). But it is possible that a serious common and fatal illness left an insufficient number of survivors to maintain the unreliable industry of agriculture. Connected to this theory is that, rather than killing the people, the plague affected, and killed off, most of the cattle.

Then there is the idea that building stopped simply because

the farmers had got tired of it (some modern thinkers have introduced the word 'stress' to describe such a situation). Perhaps they had by now realised that there was no end in sight for these buildings, and that unless the workers withdrew their labour the work would necessarily go on for ever.

And maybe by now they had a sufficient number of tools, cups, plates and cooking pots and simply did not need to make any more pottery.

A more natural explanation is that during this period there was a long and severe drought, and that the lands could no longer sustain the growing population numbers. Droughts and disappointing harvests were by no means uncommon. There is some, but not much, evidence of a prolonged series of dry years having occurred.

The exhaustion of ground fertility by intensive farming and increased soil erosion following the depletion of trees may have been additional contributory factors.

And, finally, there is the possibility that the islands were invaded. The farmers had led totally peaceful and apparently harmonious lives, with no need to make weapons. They would have been easily conquered by any warlike nation.

The Maltese archipelago is, after all strategically positioned – centrally placed in the Mediterranean from any direction. Although lacking most natural resources, it offered safe harbours and fresh water to passing vessels and their crews.

Any invaders would have been more likely to have enslaved, than to have wholly massacred, the population, but it would certainly have stopped building and pot-making.

The biggest problem of all for modern archaeology is to find an explanation for what happened during that missing 200-year period. Surviving skeletal bones show no signs of disease, starvation or warfare.

Whether the islands had been deserted and become totally uninhabited by the original settlers is unknown, although it seems unlikely.

Whatever the truth, it is unresolved. It may actually have been a combination of all (or some of) the theories.

It is as if a dark cloud passed over them, wiping out both memory and history, and leaving only dozens of mostly unfathomable ruins. The end of 'temple building' was as mysterious as its beginning.

But new people did arrive. Perhaps they were African or 'Phoenician'; maybe they were new Sicilians and maybe different races lived in harmony.

The second set of settlers may have been small in number and little is known about them except that they brought with them new influences and traditions – one of which was cremation, rather than burial, of their dead.

They almost certainly introduced the first horses.

They also brought metal.

They partially destroyed some of the monumental sites (in which they obviously had no interest) by converting them into housing, or making use of the stone to build new homes.

This was the Bronze Age, which had started in mainland Europe and northern Africa while the Gozitans and Maltese were preoccupied with stone and temples, and was about to change the face of the islands.

As wood and charcoal were required for the smelting of metals it was also going to finalise the deforestation of both Gozo and Malta.

And from that date the Gozitans (and Maltese) would produce nothing of note that all the other Mediterranean societies were not doing better.

Perhaps they did not need to. They had already made their everlasting mark on world history.

*

Further reading: books and papers

Malta: Pre-history and Temples, David H Trump.

Malta Before History, Edited and illustrated by Daniel Cilia;

Gozo: The Roots of an Island, Anthony Bonanno et al;

The Lure of the Islands: Malta's first Neolithic Colonisers, Anthony Bonanno

The Death of the Temple People, Edward Duca, *Think* magazine

The Early Mediterranean Village, John Robb

The Harbours of Ancient Gozo, Timothy Gambin

The Making of the Middle Sea, Cyprian Broodbank

The Human Form in Neolithic Malta, Isabelle Vella Gregory

Ġgantija Temples and Heritage Park, Daphne M Sant Caruana

Die Insel Malta im Altertum, Albert Mayr

The Prehistoric Antiquities of the Maltese Islands, J D Evans

A House for the Temple Builders, C Malone, S Stoddart and D Trump

Notice of a Tomb Cave at Ghain Sielem, 1884, A A Caruana

The Medical History of the Maltese Islands: Prehistory, C Savona-Ventura & A Mifsud

Gozo: The Island of Calypso: Joseph Attard Tabone

*

www.ingramcontent.com/pod-product-compliance
Lightning Source LLC
LaVergne TN
LVHW051058080426
835508LV00019B/1939